THE QUEST FOR IDENTITY AND AGENCY AS A BLACK SCHOLAR AND HUMAN RIGHTS ACTIVIST

Charles P. Henry

THE QUEST FOR IDENTITY AND AGENCY AS A BLACK SCHOLAR AND HUMAN RIGHTS ACTIVIST

Combatting Invisibility and Gaining Legitimacy

Activism and Social
Movement Studies
Collection Editor

R. Anna Hayward

LPp

First published in 2025 by Lived Places Publishing

British Library Cataloguing in Publication Data
A CIP record for this book is available from the British Library.

ISBN: 9781917503099 (pbk)
ISBN: 9781917503112 (ePDF)
ISBN: 9781917503105 (ePUB)

Cover design by Fiachra McCarthy
Book design by Rachel Trolove of Twin Trail Design
Typeset by Newgen Publishing, UK

Lived Places Publishing
P.O. Box 1845
47 Echo Avenue
Miller Place, NY 11764

www.livedplacespublishing.com

To Loretta

Abstract

I have been a part of two interrelated social movements. The first movement was a search for identity that involved place, memory, family, and the creation of Black Studies. The second movement, flowing from the first, involved civil and human rights, that is, the right to know who you are. This movement includes diaspora, global community, intersectionality, and work inside and outside government. In short, how does one overcome invisibility, gain legitimacy and agency, and find community in an individualized society with few role models?

Key words

Human rights, Black Studies, identity, non-governmental organizations, social movements, cultural diversity.

Contents

Note on language

The words Black and African American are used interchangeably.
The word Negro was used to describe Blacks until the late 1960s.

Learning objectives

- Examine how social movements become institutionalized.
- Learn the differences between positive rights and negative rights.
- Discuss how to develop a critical, but not cynical, worldview.
- Discuss the process for creating new knowledge and recovering lost knowledge.
- Learn how global networks can change power relationships.

Introduction

The focus of the memoir is my life in two movements that shaped me and that I, in turn, tried to influence. My involvement in both movements grew organically from my existence as an African American male born in mid-twentieth-century America. As I advanced in school, I increasingly looked for myself reflected in the history I read and the teachers I listened to. There was little history about African Americans and what existed was largely negative. Thus began my work in Black Studies from college to this very day.

I also continue to be involved in the movement for human rights. To be an African American youth in the 1950s and 1960s was to participate either vicariously or actively in a great awakening. It was to be a part of a struggle for human dignity and equality. I did both; that is, I participated vicariously in the Southern struggle for civil and political rights since I lived in the North and was too young to travel South on my own. Two friends and I did integrate a roller-skating rink in my hometown of Newark, Ohio, without incident during our high school years. Chapter One discusses the racism facing Blacks in the North. As I entered college in 1965, Black Power was manifesting itself in a variety of ways, including the development of Black Studies. I always saw Black Power as building on the civil rights movement rather than competing with it. The demand for civil and political rights naturally evolved into a demand for economic, social, and cultural rights. Eventually, I would teach a course entitled "Education as a Human Right" for students preparing to tutor elementary school students in Berkeley schools. My involvement in these two movements would not have been possible without the love and support of my family and several mentors.

At age 13, I decided I wanted to become president of the United States. To do so, I also decided I would need a doctorate in political science to prevent being criticized as unqualified for the position. On reflection, I believe such audacious plans must have come from two sources. The first source was my parents, Charles and Ruth, who always expected me to go to college, although neither of them had a college education. My father left school after the eighth grade, which was probably typical for a Black youth, or any youth born in 1890, especially one that was orphaned at a young age. My mother graduated from high school with a straight-A average but no hope of going to college. After all, she was a poor African American girl in the middle of the Great Depression. Through some miracle, my maternal grandparents, Lewis and Inez Holbert, saved or borrowed enough money to purchase a hundred-acre farm in the late 1920s. Although my grandfather was legally blind from working in a glass factory in Zanesville, Ohio, he learned to farm so his eight children would not go hungry. My mother walked seven miles to school every day and washed her one good dress on weekends. As a young woman, she would serve as secretary of the local NAACP. From their example, I got the idea I could be anyone I chose to be.

Photo 1 Parents Charles and Ruth Henry (circa 1966)

The second source of self-belief was external. I turned thirteen in 1960, a year that witnessed Black college and high school student sit-ins across the South and the election of a young president asking what you could do for your country. I thought politics offered a way to help the most people achieve equality and social justice. As I grew older, I retained my belief in politics as a source of social betterment; however, I decided being a politician required compromises I was unwilling to make. I got my doctorate in political science, but my desire to be president shifted toward the pursuit of facts through research and social justice through activism.

One person who listened to my dreams about studying politics and trying "to save the world" was Loretta Jean Crenshaw. We met at a summer's night yard party at the home of a girl I had dated. I was sixteen, and she was eighteen and not happy to be in Newark. Her parents, Roy and Virginia Crenshaw, her younger sisters, Rosalyn and Delores, and her brother, Roy, Jr., had recently moved to Newark from Dayton, Ohio. Mr. Crenshaw was a civilian employee of the Air Force, and his job had moved from Dayton to Newark. In the process, the Crenshaws had given up the lifestyle of a thriving Black community in Dayton for Newark's small working-class Black community. Loretta, however, was off to Wilmington College that fall and only had to endure Newark during the summer and school vacations.

It was not until I started college a couple of years later that I had any real chance of pursuing a relationship with Loretta.

I did pursue and persist and found myself happily and surprisingly married a week before my twenty-first birthday. There were doubters that the marriage would last, but as of this writing, some 56 years later, it has.

Photo 2 Loretta and Charles (1968)

Loretta taught elementary school in Newark while I finished my senior year at Denison University in Granville, six miles from Newark. When we tried to rent a house in Granville, the realtor told us someone had just taken it. The minister who married us, Reverend Charles Daugherty, sent a White couple as a test to the same realtor to ask about the rental. When they were told it was available, we had all the evidence we needed to charge them with discrimination. The realtor quickly agreed to rent to us. It would be the first of nine homes in our first fourteen years of marriage. Small wonder we have chosen to stay in the ninth home for the last forty-two years.

We decided to wait until I finished my doctorate and had a job before we had children. After a period when Loretta didn't get pregnant, we decided to adopt a newborn. There is no waiting list for Black babies, and Adia Jean entered our lives the same weekend I received my doctorate in political science from the University of Chicago in June 1974. As the first grandchild in either family, she was immediately and happily spoiled. Four years later, and still without conceiving on our own, we decided to adopt a boy. Charles Wesley, named for his two grandfathers, joined the family in the summer of 1978. Our family seemed complete when Loretta became pregnant with Laura Anne, born in August 1980. I think Loretta would agree with me that being a good parent is by far the hardest thing either of us has ever tried to do. Every child is different and presents different challenges. We have been blessed with three grandchildren. Adia has two daughters, Ashlyn and Michael, and Wes has a son, Tyler. All six have enriched our lives. My brother, Oren, and his wife, Lisa, have been supportive throughout my career.

Photo 3 The Henry Family (2017)

In addition to the support of my family, three mentors stand out among the many people who have helped me along the way. Julius Richardson was one of the Black professionals, like Roy Crenshaw, who moved from Dayton to Newark with the Air Force. Born in 1921 in Blythdale, Pennsylvania, he had joined the Tenth Cavalry at an early age and remained for twenty years supporting his family of wife Margaret and four daughters. Mr. Richardson had learned golf while in the military, played on the all-army team, and won several tournaments. He would have pursued a career as a golf professional if discrimination against Blacks had made such dreams impossible. After working on the civilian side of the military in Newark for twenty years, he began working for Metropolitan Life Insurance Company and became a full-time golf instructor.

I met Mr. Richardson at Trinity AME Church, where he taught Sunday school. My best friend, Ed Folds, lived on the same street as the Richardsons, so it was easy to visit him outside the church. He became a sort of godfather to us both. My father was raised in a generation when children were seen but not heard. According to my mother, he was not enthusiastic about having children at age 57. In short, while my brother and I knew Dad loved us, we didn't bring our problems to him or ask for advice. Ed's father was also a little remote. Mr. Richardson was from a younger generation and helped fill that gap. Since he had spent time in the Tenth Cavalry, he enjoyed talking with my father about his experience with the famous "Buffalo Soldiers" as well as his activities in the Masonic lodge.

One incident shows Mr. Richardson's laid-back style. Ed and I had recently gotten our driver's licenses and wanted to go to

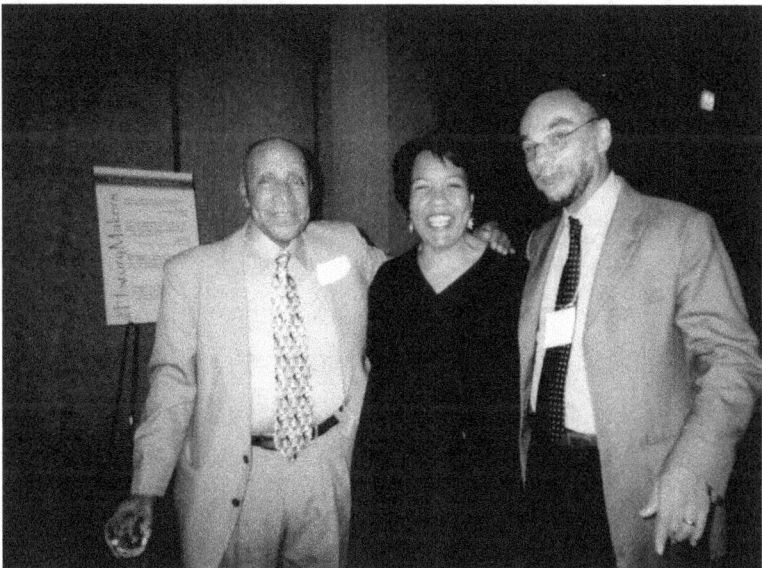

Photo 4 Julius Richardson, Julieanna Richardson, and Charles (2003)

Columbus to cruise for girls. My car wasn't running as was often the case, so we decided to ask Mr. Richardson if he would loan us his car. We went to his home early on a Saturday night. Rather than say no, he invited us in, made some small talk about sports and school, and got us to play some games. By the time we had finished, Mr. Richardson said it was too late to go to Columbus. As I grew older, I appreciated his calm demeanor and sage advice. He knew my ambitious plan for politics and was always encouraging. I only wish I had been more interested in golf as a teenager. He took Ed and me to the professional World Series of Golf in Akron, but I never expressed a desire to take it up. *Golf* magazine would later name him one of the hundred best golf instructors in the country.

I'm not sure when I first met Ginetta Sagan. She probably invited me to her home in Woodside, south of San Francisco, shortly after I was elected to the board of Amnesty International USA so she could lobby me. Of course, I accepted because Ginetta was a human rights legend. As a teenage Ginetta Moroni, she had been a part of the Italian resistance to Mussolini during World War II. Both of her parents, who were physicians, were killed, and Ginetta was eventually captured and tortured. One night before her scheduled execution, a matchbox was dropped in the cell with the word *coraggio* (courage) written inside. The next day, resistance fighters disguised as Nazi soldiers spirited her away to freedom. Her experiences led her to spend the rest of her life fighting for human rights.

After the war, Ginetta came to the United States to study, met her future husband, Leonard Sagan, and moved to the Bay Area. As an activist, researcher, and human rights educator, she founded the first West Coast Amnesty International USA (AIUSA) group and then went on to establish 75 other groups around the country. Ginetta was named honorary board chair of AIUSA and awarded the Presidential Medal of Freedom in 1996. When I returned to Oakland after my brief work with the State Department, she asked me to chair the newly established AIUSA Ginetta Sagan Fund (GSF).

The objective of GSF was to grant an award each year to a woman working for the rights of women and children in dangerous conditions. It was hoped that in addition to the cash award, the publicity might give the recipient some protection to enable them to continue their work. A group of Ginetta's friends comprised the fund's steering committee, and Cosette Thompson (who reminded me of a young Ginetta) served as a staff liaison.

Ginetta, herself, was our greatest resource. She was a champion fund-raiser for the entire human rights movement and often reminded me that there would be no programs if we were not willing to raise the funding. One clear memory is a call from Ginetta, who was going to lunch with the philanthropist Ann Getty, asking me whether to ask for $10,000 or $100,000. I replied I had no experience in dealing with billionaires', but you might as well ask for the $100,000 because the worst outcome would be $10,000. On another occasion, a wealthy donor handed her a check for $5,000. She immediately handed it back and said he could do better!

One of my fondest memories of Ginetta is our trip to the Czech Republic. My old friend John Shattuck had become the U.S. ambassador and invited her to a luncheon in her honor with Czech human rights activists. Ginetta asked me to accompany her, and I happily agreed. We toured the old Jewish cemetery in Prague, where Ginetta and Joan Baez had transferred cash they had smuggled into the country to Polish Solidarity activists years earlier.

We had lunch at a restaurant at the foot of the Charles Bridge and sat at a hidden table where a young Ginetta had had her last meal with her father. John took us to a concert, and I later played tennis with him on a court at the ambassador's residence where we were staying. He had neglected to tell me he had been taking tennis lessons from a former Wimbledon champion. The day before the luncheon, a concert in her honor took place on the lawn. The luncheon, however, produced some tension. Members of the old Communist regime were there as well as leaders of the new Havel administration. The Czech Republic had not gone through a truth and reconciliation process, and it was clear the privileges the old elite enjoyed were still resented.

After chairing GSF for several years, I suggested the group should have a female chair. Ginetta disagreed, and we settled on a female co-chair. When she passed away in 2000, it felt safe to turn the leadership over to a female chair. Loretta and I visited a bed-ridden Ginetta at the end of her life. Before we left, she insisted I take the painting of Port Elizabeth, South Africa, on the wall over her bed. She and Leonard had purchased it in South Africa many years earlier. The painting, along with an African sculpture that had belonged to her parents, which she had given me some time earlier, is among my prized possessions.

I met Bertram Gross in the mid-1980s. My research and teaching of race and public policy had led to an interest in the

Photo 5 Ginetta Sagan and Charles in Prague (circa 1997)

Hawkins-Humphrey Full Employment Act. Having worked on the staff of both Senator Humphrey and the Congressional Black Caucus, I knew the act was a key piece of legislation advancing Black economic equality in the 1970s. When I mentioned to someone that I was writing an article on the act, they said you should interview Bert Gross; he lives near Berkeley in Moraga. I did interview Bert, and by the end of the interview, he had asked me to co-author an article or book on full employment with him.

By that time, Bert was in semi-retirement while his second wife, Kusum Singh, taught at St. Mary's College. Born in Philadelphia in 1912, he had a BA and MA in English from the University of Pennsylvania. Graduating from college with no job prospects during the Great Depression, Bert joined a pro wrestling tour of South America billed as the "Jew Boy". He was not the fan favorite in Argentina. Following World War II, he worked on the Senate staff of Robert Wagner, drafting what would become the Full Employment Act of 1946. Although he lacked a degree in economics, Bert served as the first director of the president's council of economic advisors. He also worked as an economic advisor to the young Israeli government and eventually taught public administration and public policy at Hebrew University, Syracuse University, CUNY, and Wayne State University. Bert had drafted the new full employment bill at the request of Representative Augustus Hawkins and was greatly disappointed when the Carter administration failed to fully implement it. Bert's 1980 book, *Friendly Fascism*, gained him an audience on the left and an invitation to visit Cuba. The work continues to be relevant today.

I was fortunate to become one of Bert's honorary sons. There were at least eight of us who had worked with Bert over the years. He had four sons with distinguished careers by his first wife, Nora Faine Gross, and three distinguished stepdaughters by Kusum. A typical visit to Bert and Kusum would involve me giving Bert something I had written. He would look it over, say it was the best thing he had ever seen on the subject, and then offer a few suggestions for improvement. This process would repeat itself four or five times before he deemed the piece acceptable.

Photo 6 Oren Henry, Bert Gross, and Charles (1991)

'Bert was interested in my human rights work with AI and quickly absorbed most of the literature on the subject. We decided to cast full employment within the context of the larger quest for economic rights. One product of that approach is discussed in chapter 12.

This work is a memoir of my life in two social movements. My research is not discussed, but it is related to my activism. Movements have goals and methods of achieving those goals. Research can inform movements both by examining the past and predicting the likelihood of success. Social science research is less reliable than natural sciences because it has human beings as its subject. Objectivity, while often desirable, is not possible because the researcher is also a human being. The reverse is also true; an insider's view of a movement can inform those who study it. At best, one can collect as much information from as many sources as possible before reaching a conclusion. Given these limitations, I want to mention four of my publications and why I chose to write about the subject.

Culture and African American Politics was my first single-authored book. I was inspired by Lawrence Levine's *Black Culture and Black Consciousness*, an examination of antebellum and post-bellum Black culture using folklore and popular culture. The dominant schools of history in the early twentieth century used the writings of slaveowners to provide a perspective on slavery. That perspective presented the slave master as a benevolent figure and the enslaved as ignorant and lazy. An image that is still reflected in the views of some conservatives, for example, the welfare queen. There was no comparable body of work from the enslaved perspective because they were not permitted to read or write. Levine used folklore, music, and even jokes to present that perspective. To my knowledge, no one had attempted that approach in political science. My book uses those oral sources to uncover a distinct Black politics.

Another historian, John (Jack) Kirby, had written a book about Blacks in the New Deal in which he briefly mentions Ralph Bunche. In all my political science education, I had not come across his name or work despite Bunche being the first Black political scientist, the president of the American Political Science Association, the principal researcher for Gunnar Myrdal's classic *An American Dilemma*, and the first Nobel Laureate of African descent. He filled a gap in my education between the early twentieth-century debates between W. E. B. DuBois and Booker T. Washington and the modern civil rights movement. I asked Jack for biographical references on Bunche, and he said there were no biographies.

I decided to write *Ralph Bunche: Model Negro or American Other?* and edit *Ralph Bunche: Selected Speeches and Writings.*

In 2000, Randall Robinson wrote *The Debt*, an examination of the demand for racial reparations. I was surprised to find a book on this controversial subject at my local Costco. It helped revive a movement that had been around since the Civil War and General Sherman's call for 40 acres and a mule for the freedmen. When former civil rights leader and Washington insider Vernon Jordan visited Berkeley to promote his own autobiography, I asked him what he thought about the newly reenergized movement. He said he didn't think about it because it wasn't going to happen. I thought this dismissive attitude was a bit shortsighted since the same argument could have been applied to the abolition of slavery or many movements since then. I decided to write what became *Long Overdue: The Politics of Racial Reparations.*

One final publication is worth mentioning because it underlines the difficulty of objectivity in social science research. Shortly after Tom Bradley's unsuccessful bid to become governor of California in 1982, I tried to publish an article in which I claimed race was the major factor in his defeat. Bradley had lost despite the election of White Democrats to other statewide offices. Even exit polls were unreliable because some White voters were telling pollsters they voted for Bradley when the results demonstrated they had not. A *Los Angeles Times* article in 2013 concerning the role of race in the 2012 presidential election credited me as the first to write about the "Bradley effect". There was no Bradley effect for me to write about at that time; however, later writers would refer to what happened to Bradley. More interesting from my perspective was the difficulty in getting my research on Bradley published. I had called on my colleague Percy Hintzen, an expert in quantitative methods, for help in running computer regressions controlling for all the other possible factors in Bradley's defeat. In short, the research was solid, and I thought the quantitatively oriented *America Political Science Review (APSR)*, the discipline's most influential journal, might publish it. After sending it to them, I received the redacted responses from three reviewers: one said publish it, another said it should be published but not in the *APSR*, and the third said don't publish it. I sent the manuscript to another political science journal, and the reviews were almost identical to the *APSR* reviews. I then decided to send it to a Black Studies journal, which immediately agreed to publish it. Later at professional conferences, I was asked by two Black political scientists what happened to my Bradley piece. When I told them my story, they said they had reviewed it and urged publication. A lesson learned on objectivity.

1
Buckeye Lake Amusement Park

Before Six Flags, Great America, or even Disneyland, there was Buckeye Lake Amusement Park. Started in 1902, it was only about 10 miles from Newark. In fact, the interurban electric train ran from Newark to Buckeye Lake and Columbus in the early twentieth century and helped make the place a popular resort. A trip to Buckeye Lake Park was the highlight of my summer (and maybe Oren's too) for most of my youth.

The first thing you saw on leaving the parking lot ($2 admission) was a big merry-go-round, my mother's favorite ride. To its right was the big Skateland arena, but I never learned to skate, and close to it was the Pink Elephant nightclub. Once you got past those, there was a series of rides and games. My favorite ride was the bumper cars, where I loved crashing into my mom and brother. They also had a small train and children's rides in the center of the park. There was a small midway with games like darting the balloons or knocking over the pins. My favorites were a horse racing game where you competed against other players and a Skee-Ball machine that gave you coupons you could collect and cash in for big prizes like stuffed animals. It was also the first place I played miniature golf, and they had great cotton candy and caramel corn on the midway. Finally, you got to the water, where there was a giant Big Dip wooden roller coaster, a picnic point, a huge pool, and the famous Crystal dance hall.

I could never get anyone to go on the roller coaster with me, but I did make it to the Crystal dance hall years later as a college student. Many famous bands and entertainers had performed there, like Louis Armstrong, Glenn Miller, Tommy Dorsey, and Bob Hope. I saw Chuck Berry there around 1966 or 1967.

Another thrill was getting on the paddlewheel boat "Queen of the Lake". It was the largest boat I had ever been on, but I was always nervous because I couldn't swim. Still, the lake was beautiful at night with all the twinkling lights on the shore and the sound of the paddlewheel going through the water.

The origins of Buckeye Lake go back 12,000 years to the last ice age. The retreating glaciers left behind a large swamp, later named Buffalo Swamp. When the Ohio & Erie Canal was created in 1826, a reliable source of water was needed for the canal, and Buckeye Lake was dug and dammed. After the canal became obsolete, the state took over and helped develop Buckeye Lake as a tourist resort. With 35 miles of shoreline and 20 islands (one eventually owned by Wendy's founder Dave Thomas), the lake had 22 hotels and averaged thousands of visitors a day at its peak.

And therein lies the dark side of Buckeye Lake. I had always wondered why we only went to the lake once a year, no matter how much I pleaded to go more often. I also wondered why there were so many African Americans there. My father said it was his Masonic (Prince Hall) lodge that had a picnic there once a year. Only later, as an adult, did I learn that it was a segregated park that Blacks were permitted to enjoy once a year until the 1960s. In fact, in 1923, the Ku Klux Klan had a rally at the park that drew 75,000 members, and in 1925, they held a national convention there, drawing a half million Klan members, including the Grand Dragon of the five-state area, who lived in Newark. Over the years, the park suffered both natural and man-made disasters. A cyclone swept through the park in 1927, and a roller-coaster accident injured several people in 1958, as well as the collapse of a pier. An arsonist burned several buildings. After a failed attempt as a Country and Western theme park, it closed in 1970.

My family's arrival in central Ohio preceded the Klan. The Henry family was originally from Rockbridge County, Virginia. Rockbridge County got its name from a natural limestone bridge that crosses Cedar Creek. This natural bridge—over 200 feet high and 90 feet long—was a sacred landscape for the Monacan Indians. According to legend, George Washington surveyed the bridge and cut his initials into one of the interior walls. Thomas Jefferson was so enchanted by the site that he purchased the Natural Bridge and 157 surrounding acres from the Crown in 1774.

The Natural Bridge was seen as being at the edge of civilization, and Jefferson considered building a retreat there. It attracted both domestic and foreign visitors, including Patrick Henry, Sam Houston, John Marshall, and Daniel Boone. Jefferson did not build there, but he did hire a free Black man as caretaker and to record the names of his guests in a book (Macaluso, 2018, pp. 115–117).

Jefferson's Black caretaker was also named Patrick Henry. It is not known how Henry gained his freedom, but we do know that he left two wills, one freeing his wife Louisa and giving land to his unnamed children. John Henry, another free Black living in Lexington, Virginia, witnessed his will. The 1840 Census lists a William Henry with a young family living next door to Louisa Henry, who was most likely his mother. The history of this family, my antecedents, reinforces the validity of the reparations demand for both free Negroes and formerly enslaved Black folk.

Virginia's free Black population was only 4 percent of the state's total Black population, which was by far the largest of any state (Painter, 2006, p. 73). The number of free Black people was in decline, and in the wake of Nat Turner's rebellion in 1831, their situation became even more precarious. It was clear that the ideology of the Revolution as expressed in the Declaration of Independence would not include Black folk. Alexis de Tocqueville wrote prophetically, "[w]hen I contemplate the condition of the South, I can only discover two alternatives which may be adopted by the white inhabitants of those States; viz., either to emancipate the [N]egroes, and to intermingle with them, or, remaining isolated from them, to keep them in a state of slavery as long as possible. All intermediate measures seem to me likely to terminate, and that shortly, in the most horrible of civil wars, and perhaps in the extirpation of one or other of the two races" (Quoted in Malcomson, 2000, pp. 114–115).

In response to the deteriorating conditions, William Henry decided to move his family out of Virginia to New Castle, Pennsylvania. The economy there was booming because of the construction of the Erie Canal beginning in 1828. Henry had taken up barbering, and his family came to know two other families of free

Black folk as neighbors—the Normans and the Berrys. Although Pennsylvania's mistreatment of free Blacks was mild compared to Virginia's, any location on or near the Ohio River, such as southwestern Pennsylvania, was dangerous. Nightriders moved through the region, intimidating the local free Black population. William John Henry decided to seek safer ground and, following the Erie Canal, drove a wagonload of furniture to Newark, Ohio, in the late 1830s.

Ohio was the frontier, part of the Northwest Territory that excluded slavery as the country expanded westward. Yet while the Northwest Ordinance of 1787 appeared to exclude slavery, there was a loophole that permitted retaining the enslaved who had that status at the time of its passage. Moreover, states like Ohio, Indiana, and Illinois, through their "Black Laws", made it clear that free Black people were not welcome. As Ohio Justice Nathaniel Reed explained, "Black laws" were deliberately exclusionary and encouraged African Americans to leave Ohio by denying them equal rights. "[T]he laws very purpose", he said, was to keep those who remained in the state "miserable and degraded" (Weiner, 2013, p. 35).

Newark was established in 1802 on the site of ancient earthen mounds built by the Hopewell culture (recently declared a UNESCO World Heritage Site). When the Henrys moved to Newark, Ohio, along with the Normans and Berrys, there were roughly 20,000 free Black folks in the state. While Newark may have been safer than the Pittsburgh area, Blacks were not welcomed with open arms. As a young boy, Newark's most distinguished native, Edward Roye, had pleaded with the town's board of trustees not to execute an order for all Negroes to leave town within 24 hours. Trustee A. E. Elliot succeeded in having the order postponed indefinitely. Following his education in Newark's schools, Roye attended Ohio University and then taught school in Chillicothe, Ohio, and later opened a barbershop/bathhouse in Terre Haute, Indiana. After his mother, Nancy, died in 1840, the same pressures on free Blacks that drove William Henry to Newark led Roye to leave the country entirely. In Liberia, Roye became a merchant, shipowner, chief justice, speaker of the House, and the fifth president of the country in 1871.

Prior to the Civil War, William Henry set up a barbershop, bought a home, and sent his children to school. There were no public funds to support schooling for Black children, so William, John Norman, and two other free Blacks convinced the local Board of Education to build a schoolhouse on land one of them owned. Funds were raised by the board and the Black community, and a frame building was constructed, only to be torn down by unknown persons the night after its completion. It was then rebuilt, and one of the free Black supporters, Jackson Shackleford, armed himself and guarded the structure all night. Later, in 1861, a brick schoolhouse was constructed next to the Henry home (McMillan, 2002, p. 124). Prior to 1829, there were no laws formally barring African Americans from Ohio's schools, but with the establishment of public schools that year, such exclusion became formalized (Weiner, Op. Cit., p. 58).

William Henry and his wife, Elizabeth Swain, had three sons— Oren, Charles, and John. In 1864, William sent his two eldest sons off to fight with the United States Colored Troops. On his return from the war, now Sergeant Charles Patrick Henry joined his father's barbershop, but soon Sergeant Henry moved to

Coshocton, Ohio, to set up his own barbershop. Charles found that Coshocton was no more welcoming of Blacks than Newark. The *Coshocton Age* newspaper of June 27, 1885, published a threatening letter sent to Charles because of his protest of a local lynching:

> Mr. Henery (sic) the guardian of all the niggers and part of the whites of Coshocton you and all the rest of dam black nigers about the place are here by notified to leave inside of 30 days or you will be presented with as neck tie or if any of you are caught with a white woman you will get the same fait, or the blew flyes might blow you, and also the white women whoe may be caugjht with an niger will meat the same blessing. (signed) Many citizens)

My great-uncle Charles refused to leave.

Oren, who had been wounded in the Battle of Lookout Mountain, also worked as a barber in Newark until his death in 1880. The third Henry son, John, married Elizabeth Norman in 1881 and worked as a barber in Newark until his death by accident in 1898 (on the same interurban route that ran to Buckeye Lake). After Elizabeth's death by consumption in 1900, their four surviving children—Rhea, Hazel, Helen, and Charles—went to live with their Uncle Charles in Coshocton. Only Charles Patrick Henry II would survive to adulthood.

A few years after graduating from the eighth grade in Coshocton, young Charles joined Troop C of the United States Tenth Cavalry in 1909. The unit was stationed at Fort Ethan Allen in Vermont, and he served with Buffalo soldiers returning from the western

Photo 7 Civil War veteran Charles P. Henry I and Buffalo soldier Charles P. Henry II (circa 1920)

frontier and veterans of the Spanish-American War. Leaving the army as a corporal in 1912, he returned to Newark and began a forty-year career as a brick mason with the help of his uncle, Frank Norman. Over those years he became a leader of the Masonic lodge in nearby Columbus, helped fund the building of the AME church, and was the union president. In 1940 he married Zanesville, Ohio, native Ruth Holbert, and they had two sons. Charles Patrick III (the author) was born in 1947, and Oren John was born in 1953.

As presented here, this brief narrative of the Henry family addresses two myths used by opponents of reparations. First, it disrupts the dominant national narrative that White suprem- acy was a regional problem, an aberration limited to the South. Moreover, racism does not elide Black folk who are not located in the rural South or Northern cities. No one more elegantly describes the racial environment of Black people growing up in small cities and towns in Ohio and the Midwest in general than the late Toni Morrison, a native of Lorain, Ohio. Second, the Henry family narrative counters the notion that reparations are all about slavery and slavery is past. This ahistorical view seeks to distance Americans from the consequences of past and current practices that have always included free Black folk as well as the enslaved. In fact, it attempts to present Whites as the true vic- tims of movements for justice. Thus, by space and time, White Americans avoid any serious consideration of racial reparations.

What constitutes an "American" is not beliefs arrived at induc- tively and analytically but rather acquired through exposure to narratives of the American dream. These narratives are compet- itive and come through mass and social media, formal educa- tion, and informal communal and social life. Collective identity narratives associate shared meanings with some, but not other historical and contemporary actors, whose actions and purposes they interpret and relate to a vision of what unites "us" and makes us a group. These narratives do not have to be fact-based, but they must be believable to significant audiences. By naming "our" heroes and "our" enemies and our shared triumphs and trage- dies, this collective identity not only represents but also shapes how we act in the present and future (Hayward, 2013, pp. 14, 31).

My first efforts to ensure that African Americans were a part of that collective heritage occurred during my senior year in college. Black history was largely invisible during my 12 years in Newark's public schools. My mother-in-law told me that she achieved some knowledge of Black history from her Black teachers in Dayton's segregated public schools. Newark's schools were integrated, but knowledge of our past was excluded from the curriculum, and I had no teacher of color from the first through the twelfth grade (we had no kindergarten).

While there was no formal segregation, there was informal social segregation. I was the only student of color in my elementary school, and there were a handful of Blacks in junior high school. I did well academically in both elementary and junior high school. In fact, I was a member of the National Junior Honor Society and won an award for "business math". Nonetheless, my counselor scheduled me for high school courses in the non-college track. My mother noticed this and immediately requested that I be shifted to the academic (college) track. It was also the custom for graduating ninth graders to participate in what was essentially a minstrel show with White kids acting as sidemen in blackface. I was part of the all-class choir singing songs like "Dixie" and the "Camp Town Races" for the rest of the school. I was also on the high school tennis team, but the coach conveniently forgot to tell me to show up early one day for the team's yearbook picture. High school graduation featured our local Congressional Representative, John Ashbrook, giving the commencement address. Our class motto was "man alive in 65". However, Ashbrook, a member of the right-wing John Birch Society, focused on the theme of you can't change the world, so why try? At our fiftieth-class reunion, a White female alum who I did not know approached me and apologized for the many microaggressions I must have suffered as a student. She said she had only become aware of them after marrying a Black man.

By the time I was a senior in college, the world had changed dramatically. By 1965 the Civil Rights Movement was ending, and Watts announced the arrival of Black Power. College campuses were in turmoil with protests for Black Studies and against the Vietnam War. Martin Luther King, Jr., and Bobby Kennedy were assassinated, and Richard Nixon won the presidency on a platform of law and order in 1968. I married Loretta Jean Crenshaw in the same year, and my father passed away early in 1969. Still, with the help of one of my first mentors, Julius Richardson, I convinced the Newark School Board to let me teach Black history as a guest lecturer at the high school. I lectured in all five American history courses at least once a week for an entire six-week term. Since I had no teacher training, I am sure the presentation was rough, but the material seemed to hold the students' interest. Although the school board had promised to make the subject matter a part of the curriculum after I left, it was a promise unfulfilled, but I ended up teaching Black history and Black Studies for the rest of my life.

2
A child of two movements

My years at Denison were the most formative of my life. Political science and the newly created field of Black Studies would come to shape my post-Denison career, and the friends I made at Denison continue to be an important part of my life.

Like many small college campuses throughout the Midwest, with a few notable exceptions such as Antioch and Oberlin, Denison had been virtually all White until the mid-1960s. When I arrived on campus in the fall of 1965, I was the only Black male student, and there were two Black female freshmen. Political Science Professor Fred Wirt had helped recruit me by inviting me for an overnight campus visit as a high school senior from Newark. The American Commons Club (ACC) was my host. I was commuting to school because my family could not afford room and board and had support from home, but the two Black women were isolated in all-White dorms in an all-White town with no public transportation. In fact, I ran a prototype Uber shuttling fraternity brothers to and from the bars in Newark and the airport in Columbus!

Social life at Denison revolved around a dozen and a half fraternities and sororities. At least two of the fraternities had national charters prohibiting Black members—I'm not sure about the sororities. During pledge week, I went to all ten fraternity "rushes" to see if I would be barred at the door. Most were polite, but in all cases except one, I was quickly placed with a group of potential rejects. The exception was the only non-Greek fraternity on campus, the American Commons Club. Started at Denison during World War II as an alternative to the Greeks, ACC grew to several other chapters before declining again in the 1960s. I joined along with the international students, theater majors, non-jocks, and geeks that typically comprised the membership. I didn't live in the frat house, but I ate lunch there, played on the intramural sports teams, and attended their social events.

For students interested in social activism, the major organized activity revolved around the Denison Christian Association (DCA). DCA students were involved in a variety of charity and tutoring programs in the local community and connected to the National Student Association. Professor David Gibbons was the always-supportive faculty advisor for the DCA. By my junior year, I was chairing the DCA "race relations" committee, and our activities included going to White churches in Columbus, Ohio, and then going home with parishioners to discuss race relations over Sunday dinner. Since most of the DCA students were White, the theory was that Whites should be educating other Whites on these issues. But by my junior year, the focus was shifting from "race relations" to "Black Power".

A great example of the change was my class on "Race Relations". The course was taught by an older liberal sociologist and comprised about 50 White students and me. One of our texts was Milton Gordon's *Assimilation in American Life*, and a typical class involved the discussion of some current issue that ended with the professor asking me, "what do Black/Negro people think about that Chuck" (Everyone seemed to call me Chuck with no prompting from me). One day when the discussion got around to Black Power, I said, why don't we bring Stokely Carmichael to campus and ask him instead of me. Carmichael and Charles Hamilton had just published *Black Power,* and I spent a semester locating the funding and getting the commitment from the Student Nonviolent Coordinating Committee (SNCC) to bring him to campus. Unfortunately, after it had been announced in the chapel and a few days before the actual event, Carmichael backed out.

Although there were minor incidents, now labeled microaggressions, of one sort or another in other classes, the one that had the greatest impact on me was a course on "Recent African History". Given my high school education, all I knew about Africa came from shows like "Tarzan". I was excited about getting some detailed knowledge of the continent until, in one of the first lectures, the White professor—there were no Black faculty at Denison during my student days—announced that colonialism had been a good thing for Africa. To me this seemed intuitively wrong and, given what I was hearing in the news from African independence leaders, factually wrong. I didn't know enough to challenge the professor in class, but it spurred me to read up on the subject on my own. Eventually, I offered my own "recent African history" class as one of the first courses in the new, student-run experimental college. We explicitly and perhaps naively rejected asking for credit for the courses to prove we were in it for the knowledge alone. I also decided to do my senior thesis in political science on

"African Socialism". My advisor's expertise was Eastern European politics, but at least he let me work on my own.

Incidents like this had happened to the other Black students on campus, and by my junior year we numbered around 13 in a total student population of over 1800. As James Baldwin states in *Nobody Knows My Name*, "[t]he questions which one asks oneself begin, to illuminate the world, and become one's key to the experience of others. One can only face in others what one can face in oneself. On this confrontation depends the measure of our wisdom and compassion." We began to ask ourselves what kind of education we wanted and started to meet among ourselves and with sympathetic faculty, contending that we needed a Black Studies or Black culture course that would address many of these issues. In the spring of 1968, a faculty-student committee met several times to design an interdepartmental course, "Black Culture in America", and a White English professor, William Nichols, who had directed one Honors Project in Afro-American literature, was chosen to coordinate the new course.

The course was offered in the fall of 1968 with several speakers from outside the college, including Richard Lugar, then mayor of Indianapolis and an alumnus; Reverend John Frye, a Presbyterian minister who was working with the Blackstone Rangers on Chicago's south side; and Reverend Joseph Washington, a scholar on Black religion in America. The topics and the speakers were interesting enough that our Wednesday evening lectures often filled Fellows Auditorium. We discarded a plan to limit the class to twenty formally enrolled students when we saw the high quality of the written applications, and the enrollment reached sixty-seven, including all thirteen of the Black students then on campus. Because the class was large, four members of the faculty agreed to volunteer as discussion leaders, and I became a teaching assistant. In addition, several members of the faculty gave lectures. So, the Black Culture course had a great deal going for it—intense student interest, resource people from outside the college, and enthusiastic faculty participation.

From the very beginning, however, the course was marked by disappointment, anger, suspicion, confusion, recrimination, and, finally, a student boycott. Neither students nor faculty were prepared for the conflict that the course generated, and it required some serious negotiations to hold the course together through the semester. We could rationally plan the course, but we had no way of anticipating the feelings it would generate. As Ralph Ellison says, there is "an area in which a man's feelings are more rational than his mind, and it is precisely in that area that his will is pulled in several directions at the same time." He continues that his problem was "that I always tried to go in everyone's way but my own. I have also been called one thing and then another while no one really wished to hear what I called myself. So after years of trying to adopt the opinions of others I finally rebelled. I am an *invisible man*" (Ellison, prologue). The course did more than stay together; it introduced the college to a range of themes that were to become the core of Black Studies: the history of slavery; the crisis of the inner city; the development of jazz, Black theater, and Black literature; the economics of the ghetto; Black politics; and religion. If there was an embarrassing innocence in our attempt to cover such a range of material in one course, there was a refreshing humility on the part of most faculty. This field is crucially important, many admitted, but we haven't yet learned

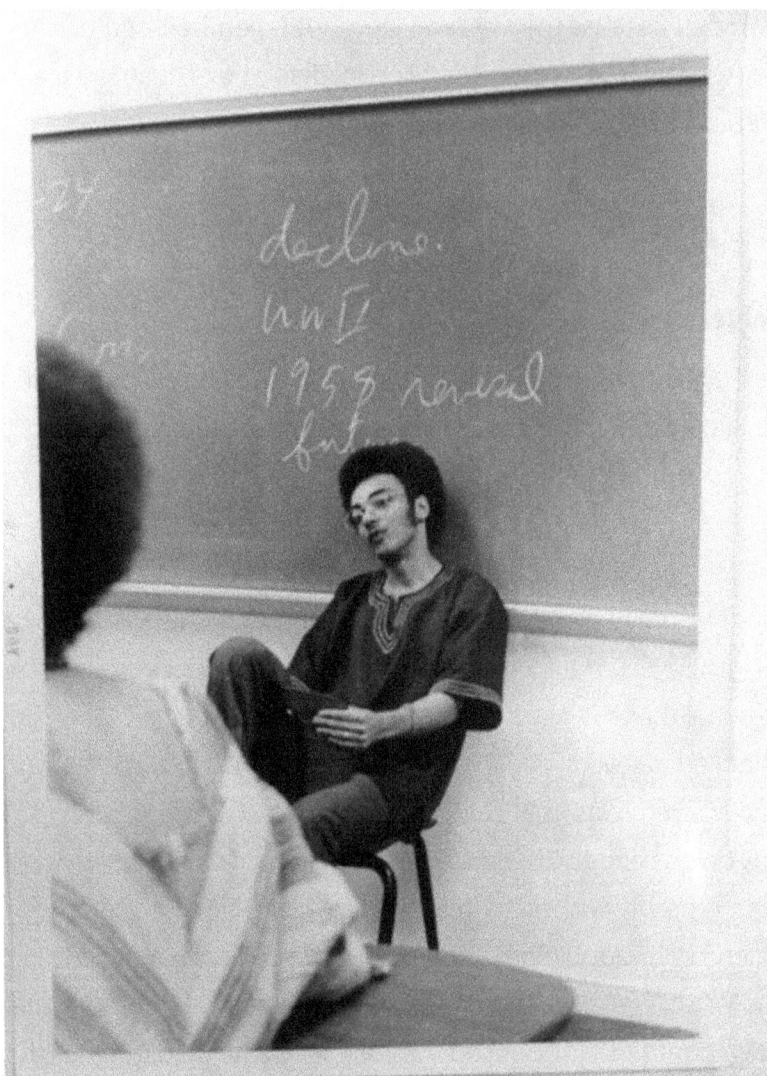

Photo 8 Charles at Denison (1968)

how to make the necessary connections, how to get beyond the limits of our own educations, and see the invisible.

Through the Denison Experimental College, we also tried to take our courses to the local community. With the local community action program (LEADS), we suggested six student-led courses: Black culture, community action and organization, basic reading and writing for adults, elementary sewing, vocational typing, and diving and water safety instruction. Four target areas were selected, and course leaders were required to undergo sensitivity training and meet with community officials to familiarize themselves with resident attitudes. I stated that our courses could "bring campus knowledge into the community and community experience onto the campus." We hoped to fully incorporate area residents as leaders in and outside the classes.

Beyond the courses, Black students at Denison began to organize. Influenced by what was happening on other campuses, we formed the Afro-American Lounge Steering Committee (AALSC), which I co-chaired, during the 1968–1969 academic year. Our chief objective was to obtain campus space to meet, study, and organize. We were successful in getting some space in a dormitory that the university agreed to remodel and furnish. I distinctly remember being given the assignment—since I had a car—to buy the stereo system for our new lounge. It was a great day when we could officially bring the music of James Brown to campus! The next year the AALSC morphed into the Black Student Union (BSU).

In 1969–1970 there was obviously no need to simulate racial conflict at Denison. The movement for Black Studies was at the center of a series of disagreements and decisions that seemed at the time to be cataclysmic. Whatever else the year meant for Denison, it established the mood within which the Black Studies program would try to develop in the next few years.

While the struggle for Black Studies erased my invisibility in the collective identity of the country and my personal identity, the Vietnam War helped me develop my moral identity. On graduation from high school, I supported the war as a fight against Communism. Unquestionably accepting the statements of our political leaders, I remember arguing with some girlfriends over our involvement. But as a political science major in college, I quickly came to question US involvement in Vietnam. Martin Luther King's speech opposing the war at Riverside Church in New York on April 4, 1967, eloquently captured my objections. His first objection was that the funds for fighting the war in Vietnam were taking away from fighting the war on poverty. Second, there was a disproportionately high death rate for Black soldiers in the war. Third, King found it contradictory to be encouraged to advocate nonviolence at home and then promote violence abroad. Fourth, he believed winning the Nobel Peace Prize gave him the responsibility to advocate for peace globally. Sixth, King believed the war was racist at its core, and he opposed imperialism. Finally, he reaffirmed his love of America and its role as an international leader that should be true to itself. (Washington, ed., 1986, pp. 233–234). Around that time, the editor of the college newspaper and I drove over 100 miles in a snowstorm to hear King at Marietta College in Ohio. It never dawned on me that the snow would also keep King from flying to Marietta from Pittsburgh.

By the 1967–1968 academic year, I was participating in the first-ever protest march against the war in my hometown. Around that time, Professor Nichols accompanied me to the draft board when I was interviewed as part of my application for conscientious objector status. Much of what I said about morality, philosophy, and religion had been absorbed from my Denison classes and guest speakers. The application was denied on the grounds that I did not oppose all wars.

It's rare that a personal milestone occurs when society itself reaches a watershed. The week marking the end of March and the beginning of April in 1968 was such a time. I was embarking on my first airplane flight, and I was terrified. A group of Denison students that included me and a faculty advisor, Professor Lou Brakeman, and his wife were flying to Puerto Rico from New York over spring break. We had our picture taken at the Pan Am terminal at JFK with a big banner that misspelled Denison (maybe a warning?).

Photo 9 Charles (far right) with Denison students

The plan was to help the locals with some simple projects during the day and party on the beach at night. What could go wrong?

Well, in the first place, the plane could crash. I decided that since I was likely to perish on this trip, I should propose marriage to the love of my life, Loretta Jean Crenshaw, just to make sure she knew how I felt about her before I met my fate. Consequently, I borrowed the money from her for an engagement ring and presented it to her at Horn's Hill Park during her lunch break from Johnny Clem Elementary School. She said YES!!! Then it was off to New York to meet my doom.

Growing up in Newark, I was asked more than once what I was— that is, was I Black, White, Indian, and so on. Turns out I look Puerto Rican. Throughout the trip, the flight attendants kept speaking to me in Spanish, assuming I was headed home. We landed in a thunderstorm, and I was certain the plane had overshot the runway when it flew over land and then back again over the water. Praise the Lord, we made it and drove to the Christian camp that was to be our home base.

It wasn't long before we were planting trees. Drawing on my father's bricklaying genes, I took particular pride in constructing a block cistern. Unfortunately, I neglected to set up a plumb line, and the result looked like an underground Leaning Tower of Pisa. It was around that time that we took a trip to El Unque, the rainforest. This was to be the highlight of the trip as things rapidly began to deteriorate.

First, we heard reports on the radio that President Johnson announced he would not run for re-election. This wasn't bad news since I had come to oppose the war in Vietnam; however, the next news from the mainland delivered by our advisor was tragic—Martin Luther King had been assassinated in Memphis, and the country was in flames. Nonetheless, a day or two later, the group decided to end our visit with a picnic on an island a mile or two offshore.

The trip out was my first time in a sailboat and the first time on the ocean. One of our group stood at the helm, looking like Washington crossing the Delaware, and then reached for a rigging line to return to his seat. I tried the same pose, but since he was taller, I missed the rigging as the boat pitched forward, and I went over the side. I don't swim well, but I invented a new stroke that got me to the surface so rapidly that my head hit the bottom of the boat. As the propeller passed just over my head and I sank deeper and deeper, it became very quiet. Managing to get back to the surface, I was quickly pulled aboard, although it seemed like it took forever for the boat to turn around.

As I was throwing up water, they asked me if I wanted to go back to shore. Not wanting to spoil the picnic, I said, let's go on to the island. I lay shivering in a fetal position on the beach for several hours until it was time to return. Our advisor, a political scientist who would later hire me to teach at Denison, along with his wife, decided I didn't look too good and took me to the nearest hospital. The good news was that health care in Puerto Rico was free; the bad news is you must wait hours to be seen by the doctor. After an X-ray, it was decided that I didn't have a concussion, and I was sleepy but on the plane to New York the next day.

After the three-hour flight, I picked up my car at JFK and proceeded to drive a car full of students 500 miles to Granville. A day or two later, I came down with bronchial pneumonia. That was the week that was!

I graduated and headed for graduate school in political science at the University of Chicago. There were many resources available to draft resisters at the university, and I was able to attend the "Chicago Seven" trial as well. I needed them. Within the year I was drafted. For me, there were two options—I had already explored teaching at Oberlin. One was to leave the country (I applied for my first passport), and the second was to go to prison (a teaching colleague of my wife intentionally broke his leg to avoid induction). Before my induction at the army center in downtown Chicago, a draft counselor/pro bono attorney urged me not to step forward when my name was called to take the oath if I passed the physical. I had some hope of failing given the accident I had at nine had crushed my left foot, and I had extensive medical records. A settlement from the accident had provided funds for my college tuition. I passed the physical and was photographed, fingerprinted, and sent home when I refused induction.

As a last resort, my draft counselor obtained a special medical examination for me through Senator Charles Percy's office. He said ninety percent of those taking this special medical examination failed. I took the same medical records to the same draft center for the special examination. I failed and was given 4-H status. The entire experience demonstrated to me the unfairness of the draft process. Those with resources and legal help, like Bill Clinton, George W. Bush, Donald Trump and me, could go on with our lives, and those without that help could not.

Freed from the stress of the draft, I could concentrate on my graduate work. Loretta taught in the Chicago public schools, including the housing projects, and came home each afternoon with her own stories. While she was engaged with almost all Black elementary school classes, I was surrounded by White faculty and students. A small group of Black graduate students in political science quickly bonded and remained lifelong friends. They included Marguerite Ross Barnett, Dianne Pinderhughes, Toni-Michelle Travis, Linda Williams, and Lorenzo Morris. I was able to take a course for the first time from a Black teacher/professor. The distinguished historian John Hope Franklin taught a course on African American history that many students from other departments, including me, enrolled in. I was impressed that Franklin read our papers and took the time to correct our grammar and spelling! The political science department had no Black professors, and some of us met with the department chair to ask why. We were told that there were very few qualified Black political scientists available. When we replied that surely some of the department's own Black graduates must be qualified, the chair promised to try to recruit faculty of color.

I had been attracted to the University of Chicago because of my interest in political theory. David Easton, the leading systems theorist, taught at Chicago, and I took two of his courses. I quickly discovered that systems theory told me nothing about what was happening in the Black political universe and decided to focus on public policy. Although I was initially concerned with his southern accent, I soon became a student of Theodore Lowi, one of the leading figures in the field. Lowi was unique in his ability to come up with interesting and creative ideas and accessible to students. Several of my fellow Black students also decided to study with Lowi. Later, I was honored to contribute to a *festschrift* honoring his career shortly before his death. When Lowi left Chicago for Cornell before I completed my dissertation, William J. Wilson agreed to serve in his place on my oral examination committee. I distinctly remember Wilson asking me how Ted Robert Gurr's *Why Men Rebel* related to my dissertation on the civil rights movement. I quickly asked him to summarize Gurr's argument since I had not read the book, and Wilson seemed satisfied with my answer. At least I can assume he was satisfied since I passed the examination!

Getting on with my life included applying for and receiving the American Political Science Association Congressional Fellowship that I had first heard about from my undergraduate political science professor, Roy Morey, who had been a fellow. Departing from the political science text during his lectures, Morey would say this is how politics really works from the inside. I wanted that on-the-ground experience.

Having completed my coursework for the doctorate in political science, I arrived in Washington, D.C., in the fall of 1972, anxious to finish writing my dissertation and excited to work on "The Hill". My wife got a job as an education consultant at one of the "infamous" K Street lobby firms, and I joined the other fellows in being briefed by the fellowship director, Thomas Mann, and reading accounts of past fellows. According to these confidential files, two of the best offices to work in on the Senate side were Senator Lee Metcalf's office and Senator Hubert Humphrey's office. I knew little to nothing about Metcalf, but, of course,

Humphrey was internationally known. I chose to apply for a position with Humphrey along with several other fellows.

On the ninth anniversary of John Kennedy's assassination, I had a meeting with his chief opponent for the Democratic presidential nomination in 1960, Hubert Humphrey. Humphrey had served as vice president under Lyndon Johnson and had just returned to the Senate after losing one of the closest presidential elections in history to Richard Nixon in 1968. After a few years out of political office, Humphrey returned to Washington as the junior senator from Minnesota (Walter Mondale was the senior senator). He conducted the interviews for two fellows' positions on his staff.

Even though Humphrey was a civil rights hero to liberal Democrats based on a famous human rights speech he gave at the 1948 Democratic National Convention and his steadfast support for civil rights as mayor of Minneapolis and in Congress. I, however, disagreed with his support for the war in Vietnam. Although Humphrey, himself, had some doubts about United States involvement, he went along with Johnson to gain his support for the presidential race in 1968. Given Humphrey's support, I voted for the Peace and Freedom Party candidate for president, comedian/activist Dick Gregory.

I got one of the two positions in Humphrey's office after his first choice, British journalist William Shawcross, turned down the offer to work for Senator Ted Kennedy. Later I discovered that Shawcross was placed in an annex office and seldom saw Kennedy, while I was seated with Humphrey's legislative assistants and saw him nearly every day. I was quickly given responsibility for the reintroduction of ten bills in January. This included responsibility for

legislation in the Public Works and Commerce Committee, especially the Highway Trust Fund and Congressional Reform. On this
latter topic, Humphrey had given one of his earliest speeches in
the Senate on the need to eliminate the Committee on Non-
essential Expenditures. He was roundly condemned as out of line
for such a suggestion! My work also included advising on co-
sponsoring bills and writing statements for the co-sponsorships
and overseeing Humphrey's many interns—I had my own intern!
I told our administrative assistant that I was a little nervous advising the senator on which bills to support given my lack of experience. He said not to worry because Humphrey would know if
the advice was wrong—this was not the case for many senators.
Humphrey had a deep knowledge of topics as varied as nuclear
disarmament, agriculture, and civil rights. He also knew personally the leaders of the Soviet Union, all the major farm groups,
and the leaders of the major civil rights organizations.

While he was only the junior senator from Minnesota, Humphrey
was considered a national senator. That is, his constituency was
nationwide, not just statewide. He sent out roughly 300 to 400
letters a week and was always on the phone. I answered many
of the letters sent to the senator that required more than an
automatic response (robo letters). The responses ranged from
bank presidents and airline executives to average citizens with
complex questions. You never knew who might drop by the
office. John Glenn, Hollywood actors, and Minnesota constituents were among the visitors. Those that did not get a meeting
with the senator were often directed to me or another legislative assistant. Some were pleased to get a hearing while others
were upset they couldn't talk to the senator. I also had to handle

phone calls to the office about a wide variety of topics. Of course, many wanted to talk with Humphrey but had to settle for me. Some wanted to lecture me, and some had simple questions like, why was a pound of chicken 39 cents last week and 59 cents this week?

One of my favorite duties was accompanying Humphrey when he gave speeches to the many student groups visiting the Capitol. He and Muriel (his wife) had decided that that would be one of his chief activities during this phase of his career. He enjoyed this engagement with young people, and I often had to pull him away to take him to his next meeting. Usually, they wanted to take pictures and get his autograph, and he would always oblige. Sometimes I would be sent ahead to entertain an audience while they waited for the senator to arrive. Here is my diary entry for February 15, 1973:

> Had a surprise meeting with some high school students from Minnesota. I held them until both Humphrey and Mondale showed up. They had already talked with Representative aides and the Pentagon. The Pentagon aide said he didn't know the defense budget figures when they asked him. Humphrey talked and Mondale listened to him for over half-an-hour. Humphrey waxed eloquent over cuts in poverty programs while aid went to Vietnam. The president had broken the law like the draft dodgers he condemns. He had the students crying and got choked up himself…

Humphrey worked seven days a week and expected his staff to be on call or in the office when he needed them. He had remarkable energy for a man his age or any age.

Former President Harry Truman died in December 1972. Humphrey was asked to give one of the eulogies at his funeral. Apparently, he and Truman were good friends because the family gave Humphrey one of Truman's walking canes after the funeral. A month later, Lyndon Johnson died. Of course, Humphrey knew Johnson well and did media interviews all day. Humphrey took Marty, the other Congressional Fellow, and me up to the family gallery in the Senate to watch the eulogies being presented on the Senate floor. I was able to bring my brother, Oren, and Loretta with me. Later we watched the Johnson funeral procession enter the Capitol on a bright, cold January day.

A highlight for me was the meetings with the other Congressional Fellows at lunch, receptions, or frequently at talks by politicians, political scientists, and journalists to our group. I got Humphrey to speak, and naturally, he was well-received. A few fellows met to consider writing a book about our experience. The problem was that our insider knowledge was what we had to offer, but we agreed anything too revealing would destroy our boss's trust in the fellowship program. The idea was abandoned. One former fellow I had lunch with was my old undergraduate professor, Roy Morey. He was now working in the Nixon administration and said there might be a place in the Republican administration for me when the fellowship was over if I was interested. Morey went on to a distinguished career as a senior officer in the United Nations Development Programme.

Perhaps the biggest highlight for me was the late evenings when Humphrey could relax and tell stories about his many experiences. He was always in a good mood when he returned from foreign travel, where he was welcomed by world leaders. One of my favorite anecdotes involved the time he stayed at Windsor Palace in the private residence. He said tricycles and toys were strewn all over the place, and Princess Anne had asked him to convince her mother, the Queen, to let Anne attend a co-ed school. Another highlight was a trip with Humphrey on a Bell Labs jet to their New Jersey laboratories. We were escorted the whole time by two of their lobbyists and shown some of the latest technology. I'm not sure whether Humphrey or I fully comprehended the presentations, but it was an interesting experience. One thing I noticed as we traveled was his frequent trips to the restroom, unfortunately often followed by people who recognized him. He was in the early stages of bladder problems that would claim his life a few years later.

One day at a staff meeting in early January, Humphrey asked me what I thought of his idea on a resolution declaring Congress should share responsibility with the President regarding war powers. The idea came from his experience with Vietnam. I told him I didn't have an answer, and he said, think about it. We had come full circle.

Photo 10 Charles and Hubert Humphrey (1973)

3
Washington, DC: The caucus and the capstone

Washington is the perfect location for someone interested in American politics. I took full advantage of the location by attending Congressional hearings, Supreme Court sessions, lectures for APSA Fellows by distinguished journalists and politicians, Hill receptions, and frequent lunches with other Fellows. I also found time to do some dissertation research at the Library of Congress. After all, the fellowship would end by fall, and I needed a job. To that end, I made my first trip to California for two job interviews.

The University of California at Santa Cruz (UCSC) invited me for a job talk, and I managed to tack on a secondary trip to San Diego State University (SDSU) for an additional interview. Loretta and I flew into San Francisco, rented a car, and drove to Santa Cruz. The campus was gorgeous. It was new, decentralized, and nestled in the redwoods overlooking the Pacific Ocean. Instead of departments, there were clusters of faculty housed in separate colleges with different themes. Grading involved written evaluations rather than grades, and the whole atmosphere was informal. In short, the opposite of the University of Chicago. Unfortunately, things were so informal they seemed to have difficulty gathering faculty to hear my talk and had no one for Loretta to talk to. We left Santa Cruz unsure about how we would fit in there and drove south.

San Diego State and my host, Charles Andrian, seemed more organized and more energized about having me there. The San Diego area was beautiful but also conservative. We were told housing with ocean views was available and affordable. The drawback with SDSU was the teaching load of three courses a semester compared to two at UCSC. I wanted time to do research and publish, which ultimately led me to favor Santa Cruz. Before a decision could be made at UCSC, however, a budget freeze went into effect, leaving me still on the job market.

On April 23, 1973, I went to work with the Congressional Black Caucus (CBC). They were happy to add a Congressional Fellow to a very small staff. Although the Caucus had been formed in 1970, it was still in the process of finding space and figuring out its institutional role. The executive director was Augustus (Gus) Adair, a Black political scientist from Morgan State College in Baltimore. Gus had been Representative Parren Mitchell's campaign manager, and I imagine the CBC job was his reward. Gus was funny, direct, and seemed to know everyone in the Black political universe. There were a few additional staff and a secretary. It would be a month before we moved into permanent space at the old Congressional Hotel.

Communication between the CBC staff and members' staff was poor. An early example occurred when Gus sent out a memo urging members to vote against an extension on the western front of the Capitol as too expensive at a time when poverty programs were being cut. Members appreciated Gus's initiative since his predecessor apparently spent a great deal of time collecting speakers' honorariums. Unfortunately, Gus had not cleared the statement with CBC Chair, Louis Stokes (D-OH) of Cleveland. A successful lawsuit by my cousin, Charles Lucas, had created the 21st Congressional District represented by Stokes. My cousin had run for the seat but was a Republican in a Democratic city. Andrew Young and Barbara Jordan had followed Gus's advice but were surprised when the rest of the Caucus voted for the extension. They were not aware of a deal reached a year earlier in which Ron Dellums (D-CA) received a seat on the Armed Services Committee in exchange for CBC support of the extension. Stokes voiced his displeasure with Gus.

Unfortunately, Gus and the rest of us spent a lot of time on low-level chores. The office lacked basic reference material like the *National Journal* and *Congressional Quarterly*. We had to fight to gain the use of the Congressional Research Service, which member offices routinely had. A lot of paperwork was involved in getting a few dollars for anything from donuts to printing. It was a struggle to get Congressional identity badges, and CBC staff could not attend Caucus meetings. Clearly, the members would have to get used to an active staff, but first, they needed to figure out their own role.

Part of the reason for the disorganization in staffing the CBC rests with the Ford Foundation or, more precisely, competition for Ford Foundation funding from the Joint Center for Political Studies (JCPS). Both the Caucus and JCPS applied for Ford funding at the same time. When Ford indicated it would fund only one of the applicants, the CBC withdrew its application with the understanding that JCPS would become the legislative arm of the Caucus. Under the leadership of Frank Reeves and later Eddie Williams (a former Congressional Fellow), however, the Joint Center became completely independent of the CBC. This conflict created poor relations between Reeves and the Caucus as the latter scrambled to staff its office.

Under its founding chair, Representative Charles Diggs (D-MI), the CBC filled a historic gap in directing attention to United States foreign policy toward Africa. As chair of both the Caucus and the House Subcommittee on Africa, Diggs was in a perfect position to question US support for the undemocratic and racist regimes in Southern Africa. When the United States had refused to send official observers to the 1955 Bandung Conference of "third world" leaders, Representative Adam Clayton Powell had attended as a private citizen. He questioned the wisdom of any country ignoring a meeting representing more than sixty percent of the world's population. Since the formation of the CBC in 1970, Black representatives were very active in African-related conferences, including the African American Dialogue and the African American Representatives Conference. Diggs, along with John Conyers (D-MI), Charles Rangel (D-NY), and Stokes, attended the latter conference in Lusaka, Zambia.

While the CBC would continue to play an important role in influencing US policy toward Africa, foreign policy was not a priority for the constituents of most CBC members. Police brutality, on the other hand, was an issue that was hard for members to ignore, especially when local authorities were unresponsive or complicit. This was the case on December 4, 1969, when a special unit of the Chicago police working with the FBI and district attorney raided the apartment of Black Panther leader Fred Hampton, killing him as he slept in bed along with fellow Panther leader Mark Clark and injuring four others who were in the apartment. While the police claimed the Panthers fired first, the evidence proved otherwise. The Panthers conducted tours of the murder scene, and thousands, including Loretta and me, visited the site. Visitors also included five representatives—Stokes, Diggs, Powell, Conyers, and William Clay (D-MO). These five members, joined by Panther leaders Bobby Rush and David Hillard, held a nearly six-hour public hearing on Chicago's West Side to hear community concerns over the shootings. Representatives Shirley Chisholm (D-NY) and Augustus Hawkins (D-CA) also declared their support for the Panther version of the incident. More than a decade of legal wrangling and investigations would ultimately result in a nearly $2 million settlement with the estates of Hampton, Clark, and Panther survivors of the incident. It would also mark the beginning of the end of the Daley machine.

In December 1969, the Black members of Congress had formed the Democratic Select Committee, the predecessor to the CBC, which would follow shortly. Thus, the first role of the CBC might be said to investigate police misconduct. Police oversight, however, was not a role most members were comfortable with. In late April 1972, a representative of Bobby Seale called Gus in an effort to set up an emergency national meeting in Oakland. The focus of the meeting was to discuss "issues" in the presidential election, but Jesse Jackson was the only national figure to respond favorably.

It was not the Panther hearings but rather a meeting with Richard Nixon that brought the Caucus its first national attention. From almost the beginning, the 13 members of Congress that composed the CBC sought an audience with President Nixon. Seeing themselves as the voice of 25 million African Americans, they believed the issues that concerned Blacks and the poor were not partisan issues. It was not, however, until they threatened to boycott Nixon's 1971 State of the Union address that the White House consented to a meeting. On March 25, 1971, the CBC presented 61 recommendations to Nixon covering a wide range of topics. While the overdue response from the White House was largely a declaration of the progress made under Nixon, the Caucus had gained the public's attention. In subsequent years, the Caucus would produce its own Black State of the Union message.

The need for information to refute Nixon administration assertions made the need for CBC staff obvious. Consequently, its first fundraising dinner in June 1971 provided resources for the hiring of seven staff members, including Howard Robinson, a former State Department professional, as executive director. From July 1971 to September 1972, the CBC conducted several conferences and three hearings. While this type of activity provided the Caucus with symbolic visibility, it produced little in terms of legislation. In fact, Gus and our legal counsel, Mitch Dasher, told me that members had little experience or expertise in drafting, introducing, and passing legislation. Moreover, Gus mentioned meetings with administration officials Roy Ash and Fred North concerning civil rights enforcement in which members were poorly prepared. They were no better prepared for a meeting with Democratic leader Bob Strauss on committee appointments. The end of symbolic politics came with the National Black Political Assembly (NBPA) conference in March 1972 (see Chapter 7). At Gary, the competing demands of Black nationalists, civil rights leaders, and Black elected officials proved too diverse to be captured in a single Black Agenda. By breaking with the Gary Declaration, the CBC was signaling its move from symbolic to substantive politics.

While I think the shift toward policy was overdue, it is easier to gain agreement on symbolic politics than substantive issues. On the funding of community action programs (CAP), for example, members were split. Some supported this funding for local community action agencies, while others saw this as funding potential political rivals. Organizations like the Urban League offered to work with the CBC on issues of mutual interest, and I attended one of their national conferences while on the staff. The effort to hold legislative workshops before the annual CBC dinner was aimed at building issue alliances and educating the public. Gus gave me the responsibility of coordinating the first legislative workshop. The highlight for me was putting together a presentation by Hubert Humphrey and Augustus Hawkins on their full employment bill. It gave me a chance to reconnect with friends in Humphrey's office, and the bill became a caucus priority that eventually passed after Humphrey's death as the Full Employment and Balanced Growth Act of 1978.

A much lower visibility role for the CBC was as an advocate for Black employees in the federal government. During my short time on the staff, we were approached separately by Black US Marshalls and by Black employees of the Library of Congress.

Both groups claimed they had faced discrimination on the job. It is not widely known that the civil rights legislation enacted by Congress does not apply to Congress itself.

At some point in the spring, I discovered that Howard University's political science department had an opening. I applied for the position and was granted an interview on May 31st. From the interview, I learned that departmental politics were complicated, but the students were good overall. The department chair was out of town, but I had lunch with Lee Calhoun, with whom I would subsequently share an office. Lee was finishing his first year at Howard after graduate school at the University of Michigan and was born in Toledo, Ohio, on the day before my birth in Newark, Ohio. Gus called Robert Martin, a Howard political scientist who had once been the teaching assistant of Alain Locke, to recommend me. It helped that Martin also held a doctorate from the University of Chicago.

On June 19th, Gus told me that Ron Walters said I was hired at Howard. My hiring was confirmed at about 5 pm that day— what a relief! On July 10th, I had lunch with Walters, who told me Charles Harris was returning to the department after two years leave at the Library of Congress. Walters added that I would be eligible for tenure in three years. At some point that spring, Gus had offered me a full-time job with the Caucus staff. Given my interest in research and the tenuous position of CBC staff, I turned him down. However, by accepting a position at Howard, I was able to work part-time for the Caucus the following year. Finishing the dissertation, developing new courses, and working with the Caucus meant I had a challenging year ahead.

There were several good reasons for staying in DC besides politics. The astounding diversity of the area presented many opportunities for cultural enrichment. Of course, the many museums of the Smithsonian were free, and major productions were always playing at the Kennedy Center. Biking or hiking along the B & O Canal was popular, as was the political comedy of Mark Russell.

Unfortunately, all these attractions meant DC was expensive to live in. Our first year found us renting an apartment in the Arlington Towers with a view of the Iwo Jima Memorial right outside our front room window. At the end of our first year, the apartments went on sale as condos, and we had to look for something more affordable. Our income meant we had to pass up some great real estate deals on Capitol Hill, and we ultimately ended up buying a townhouse in District Heights, Maryland.

Another reason for staying was the chance to teach at a Historically Black College/University (HBCU). Having been the only or one of the only Blacks in every school I attended, it felt good to be in the majority for a change. Howard was one of the few HBCUs with a full set of doctoral programs (plus a law school and medical school), which meant, at least in theory, it was research oriented. Loretta enrolled in a master's in reading program at the School of Education. Howard was sometimes called the Harvard of HBCUs, but the reality was somewhat different.

Founded in 1867, Howard was named after Union Army general Oliver O. Howard, head of the Freedmen's Bureau. A major task of the Bureau had been the education of the recently enslaved, although Whites and others were also welcome in Freedmen's Bureau schools. Thus, Howard was unique among HBCUs in that it was financially supported by the federal government rather than the private funding of most of the HBCUs, which were generally established by denominations of the Black church. This federal support, plus its location in Washington, made it attractive to the best of the first generation of Black scholars who were confined by segregation to teaching at Black schools. These scholars included Ralph Bunche, Carter Woodson, E. Franklin Frazier, Charles Wesley, Charles Hamilton Houston, Sterling Brown, Alain Locke, Ernest Just, Percy Julian, and Leo Hansberry, among others. These scholars, in turn, attracted some of the best African American students, including Zora Neale Hurston, Kenneth Clark, David Dinkins, Kwame Ture, Toni Morrison, and Kamala Harris.

But the similarity with Harvard ended with some of the best faculty and students. As an HBCU, Howard accepted significant numbers of students who would not have been admitted to your average state university, let alone Harvard. This policy of uplift created a real teaching challenge in trying to maintain the interest of the best students while literally helping some others to read and write at a college level. I joined three other new junior faculty in demanding high standards while trying to offer support. There was a lot of complaining when we refused to accept *Jet* magazine as a reference source!

Faculty politics at Howard were complicated, to say the least. Starting with congressional oversight of the university, Howard presidents sought to keep firm control over any kind of protest that might jeopardize federal funding. Administrators at HBCUs already had more power than predominately White universities. I saw the power dynamic at work during one of the first political science department meetings. One faculty member after another rose to denounce our new chair, Ron Walters. This caught me by surprise since my interactions with Walters had been pleasant. Later I would discover that Walters had been inserted as chair by the dean over the objections of the faculty. A situation that would have been unthinkable at Denison or the University of Chicago.

The political science faculty itself numbered 26 with numerous factions. At least two of the African American professors dated back to Ralph Bunche's tenure as chair in the 1930s. However, I was once again surprised that a majority of the tenured faculty were not African American. They would be deciding whether the four new junior faculty would receive tenure. Additional faculty included three Nigerian professors, three West Indian professors, a White South African who had represented the Bantu people in parliament, a Greek who had helped to write the fascist constitution, a radical Yugoslavian professor, and a few more senior Black faculty not associated with any faction. In short, faculty meetings could be a mind-bending experience, with one lasting eight hours.

Unlike most universities, which seek to protect junior faculty from being overburdened with administrative duties so that they can concentrate on research leading up to tenure, Howard seemed to exploit junior faculty. Perhaps it was because a Ford Foundation grant had made it possible for the department to reduce the course load from four classes to three classes per semester that we were seen as having spare time. After all, the course load was five a semester during the 1930s. In any case, my junior colleagues and I were initially impressed that we were given such responsibilities. One junior colleague was asked to take over as undergraduate advisor while I was assigned as chair of the graduate admissions committee. This came after I had just completed my own graduate work. In addition, several of us decided to redesign the undergraduate curriculum to more closely align with our graduate courses. We received no course release time for our administrative work, and no research funds were available.

Just after finishing my first year at Howard in June 1974, I received my doctorate in Chicago. That same weekend, Loretta and I rushed back to DC to meet our new adopted daughter, Adia Jean. Adia was two weeks old, and, of course, our lives were changed forever. Loretta had quit her job as an educational consultant a few months earlier to prepare for Adia's arrival. Both grandmothers came to visit to support the new parents and welcome the first grandchild in either family.

I had taken on a part-time job with the CBC to keep us financially afloat. That job ended abruptly in the summer of 1974 when Gus left the CBC. Charles Rangel (D-NY), the new Caucus chair, asked me to fill in as they conducted a search for a replacement. I said I would be happy to for a bump in pay. When Rangel declined the raise, I asked that I at least be given the title of acting executive director. When that too was refused, I ended my association with the CBC. The next year, I added a course in the honors program at the University of Maryland to my teaching load and followed that with summer school teaching at Howard.

Despite all our administrative work and teaching, my junior colleagues and I received no raise over the first two years. After each academic year, the political science faculty had ranked those deserving raises by quartiles, and each year we had been in the top quartile. When the raises were distributed, however, we found the dean's old friends in the bottom quartile with the raises. The four of us decided we needed to meet with the dean of social science for some clarification. In an unforgettable meeting, the dean said since we all had degrees from fine institutions, he was sure we could find employment elsewhere. Moreover, he added that he could hire young White faculty for less than he was paying us. Three of the four "young Turks" (including me) immediately made plans to leave the "Capstone of Negro Education".

4
Homeward bound

Once the decision had been made to leave Howard, it didn't take long to find a new, or rather, old home. One of my former political science professors at Denison, Lou Brakeman, had become provost. He invited me to return to my alma mater as director of the Black Studies Center and assistant professor of political science. Since Black Studies at Denison was a program rather than a department, my tenure track would be in political science. The salary was more than I was making at Howard, and at least I would get some course release for my administrative work. To sweeten the deal, Denison offered me a house to rent with an option to buy in the "faculty ghetto". My home would be three backyards away from campus—my best commute ever. The offer plus the urging of family to bring our young daughter to be spoiled made it an easy decision.

Black Studies had fallen on hard times in the years after its creation. The university, like many other schools, had hired a non-academic, a minister, to run the program. He, in turn, had hired his wife as his secretary and his daughter (a Denison student) as an office assistant. Lacking academic credentials, the reverend, and consequently the program, lacked credibility on campus. Brakeman believed my return would change all that, and I hoped to prove him right. It was tough to leave Washington for the village of Granville, Ohio, where we were the only Black family. The month before our departure, we witnessed a spectacular fireworks show on the National Mall celebrating the country's 200th birthday. We had also witnessed the inauguration of Richard Nixon in 1973 and his departure after Watergate as well as Lyndon Johnson's funeral procession to the Capitol.

It had been seven years since we left Granville for Chicago. My return attracted some local interest as the Newark newspaper published a picture of me addressing the faculty senate. It's always interesting and sometimes uncomfortable to establish peer relationships with your former professors. As might be expected, my strongest friendship developed with my former English teacher, Bill Nichols, who had supported the development of Black Studies at Denison and personally supported me in opposing the draft. Bill and I would later co-teach a course together on "Politics through Literature". He was a part of a small but great group of young faculty comprising the advisory committee for the Black Studies program. They all taught courses cross-listed with the program. In addition to Bill, the two faculty members I would work most closely with over the coming years were Reverend John Jackson, who was assistant dean of the university chapel, and Professor Jack Kirby of the history department.

The first year I taught both introductory Black Studies courses and political science courses. At the end of the year, I was also asked to serve as assistant dean of the college. This assignment meant that I was the only Black face at an endless stream of administrative meetings. Denison students knew little Black history, and the strong fraternity/sorority system gave them limited opportunities to interact at the social level with Black students.

The result was a continuing series of microaggressions that sometimes escalated to more serious conflict. I decided that a part of the solution would be to require every student to take a general education course in Black Studies.

This idea found enthusiastic support in our advisory committee, but we quickly realized the need for additional allies to make it happen. Inspired by the establishment of Black Studies at Denison, Women's Studies had been developed in the years I had been absent. Since there were not nearly enough Black Studies faculty to offer the courses needed to fulfill a general education requirement, Black Studies and Women's Studies faculty, led by Ann Fitzgerald and Nancy Nowick, joined together to propose that either subject could fulfill the requirement. Unfortunately, there was no faculty expertise in Latino/a Studies or Native American Studies, which prevented us from including them. After the usual objections of overburdening students with general education requirements, taxing resources, and discriminating against other racial/ethnic groups, we succeeded in establishing a Black Studies/Women's Studies general education requirement the following year. Denison would become one of the first colleges in the country to enact such a requirement.

Denison also played a part in supporting a regional and national network of Black Studies programs and departments. Fellow Black political scientist William "Nick" Nelson invited me to join the host committee planning the first annual convention of the National Council for Black Studies (NCBS). This organization had been founded by Dr. Bertha Maxwell-Roddy at a meeting she convened at the University of North Carolina at Charlotte in

1976. Ohio State University's Black Studies Department, chaired by Nelson, had agreed to host the first national conference, and I was excited to meet other colleagues building the new field of Black Studies. Chicago Mayor Harold Washington was the keynote speaker, and I was elected to the NCBS Board as a midwestern representative. This election would mark the beginning of a life-long association with NCBS in which I would coordinate the national student essay contest, host a national conference, and serve as the board secretary and board president.

As a regional representative on the NCBS board, I helped form a Great Lakes College Association (GLAC) and an Ohio Consortium of Black Studies programs. I believed it was particularly important for Black Studies programs on small campuses like Denison's to tap into a network of scholars and activists for ideas on curriculum development, research and publishing resources, and accreditation. This last process was critical since none of the traditional accrediting agencies had experience with Black Studies. NCBS offered to establish program legitimacy, and I invited two Black administrators, John Walters of Bowdoin College and NCBS Executive Director Joseph Russell of Indiana University, to Denison to review our program. Their recommendations strengthened our program and supported our legitimacy on campus.

It was at a GLAC meeting hosted by Denison that I met our keynote speaker Robert Chrisman, publisher of *The Black Scholar* (*TBS*) journal. Robert would become a lifelong friend, and I had many opportunities to publish in his journal. Robert had been on the faculty at San Francisco State University along with Nathen Hare as they pioneered the creation of the first Black Studies program, and *The Black Scholar*, founded by Chrisman and Hare, became the preeminent journal in the field. Publishing in *TBS*, however, did not carry the same weight as publishing in a peer-reviewed academic journal. Chrisman and Hare decided that in addition to publishing the work of academics, they would also include activists, the imprisoned, and third-world leaders. Thus, in many ways, it was the voice of the Black Power movement rather than solely an academic journal. I learned more about its reputation later when I agreed to publish my political biography of Jesse Jackson with *The Black Scholar Press*. When it came time for a promotion review of my work at Berkeley, the external review committee refused to give me full academic credit for a book published by *TBS* rather than a university press. At another GLAC meeting at Earlham College, I heard Florence Howe address the development of Women's Studies and Barbara Smith discuss the role of Black women in Women's Studies. Both talks provided important insights for the emergence of Black Women's Studies and Queer Studies.

Denison also provided me with my first opportunity to do some editorial writing. In 1980 I offered to write one or two columns a month for Ohio's leading African American newspaper, the *Call and Post*. Circulated in Cleveland, Columbus, and Cincinnati, I saw the newspaper as an instrument of public education and debate. For nearly two years I wrote a column called "Perspective on the Eighties" on subjects ranging from busing and the death penalty to United States foreign policy toward Africa.

In January 1977, the month Alex Haley's *Roots* was shown to a record-breaking audience on television, Loretta and I had our first chance to travel to Africa. Specifically, we were going to the Second World Black Arts Festival (FESTAC) in Nigeria. To get there, we agreed to co-lead a group of Denison students for their January term project.

The other leader of the tour was Olu Makinde, a theater lecturer at Denison who was a native Nigerian and responsible for making arrangements for the group. The problem, however, was that Olu had not been home for eight years, and things had changed. Inflation had occurred, and we only took about half the cash we needed. In addition, due to slow mail service, we had not received confirmation of accommodation at any of the places that Olu had contacted. These were universities rather than hotels, which were either much too expensive or too sketchy.

The second problem was our students. There were nine, and none of them had traveled outside the United States. They were in for culture shock and unprepared or unwilling to deal with it. There were no fast-food restaurants or hotel chains. Roads were bad, and electricity was sporadic. Thus, from the start, we had an unhappy group of campers. We were to tour the country for a couple of weeks before heading back to Lagos (where we had arrived) for FESTAC. Here is my journal entry about halfway through the trip:

> I have reached a breaking point. One of our male students has punched a female student in the eye and she refuses medical treatment. Another student has said he wants to commit suicide by not taking his malaria pills. Everyone is on a jagged edge ready to blow-up, but we are trapped. Our plane tickets have been stolen (by Olu's brother who likes one of our students and doesn't want her to leave) and we are an ocean away from home.

On another occasion, Olu, Loretta, I, and two students traveled to Ikere to visit the Oba (natural ruler) who had agreed to an audience. On the way through town, one of the students jumped out of the van and said he wanted to climb a nearby mountain. We urged him to get a guide from the Oba, but he took off without one. The Oba was young and very informal. He gave us a tour of the compound and posed with us in ceremonial robes.

While we were talking, an aide approached and whispered in his ear. The Oba told us a stranger had been spotted climbing a sacred mountain, and the townspeople were very upset. We mentioned to him our student's expedition and went outside to look and saw a tiny figure near the top. The Oba said if we had asked for his permission to climb, he would have forbidden it because the climb is dangerous and the mountain guarded by a (mythical?) giant python was only climbed once a year by a

Photo 11 Charles and Denison student with Oba (1977)

religious leader. Fortunately, the Oba sent word to the townspeople to leave the crazy American alone. When we saw our student again at dinner, he claimed people were cheering for him when he got off the mountain. We told him those were not cheers!

After several other adventures, we cut the trip short and headed back to Lagos. FESTAC was in chaos as many of their new official vehicles had been stolen. We were put in unfinished dorm-like rooms with no air-conditioning or mosquito netting. To get to any venue or dinner, we had to secure a car with a driver and armed guard. On the way to one venue, our guard beat a truck driver whose vehicle was blocking our way. After a couple of days of this, I got a car, a driver, and a guard to take me to a communications center in the city to make an international telephone call. I called my brother and instructed him to contact Denison's president and say we needed emergency airplane tickets to come home. If he failed to get President Good, I told him to call Hubert Humphrey and plead for my rescue. Before we left for the airport the next day, Olu returned with our tickets after tracking down his brother. When we flew out, the airline never told us we also had new tickets reserved for us from Denison. When we made an overnight stop in Paris, our students complained they didn't like French ice cream!

Besides *Roots*, or uproots in our case, Africa became a hot topic on campus when Reverend Leon Sullivan of Philadelphia published his seven principles of corporate responsibility for corporations doing business in South Africa in 1977. The so-called Sullivan Principles called for businesses to adopt policies of equal treatment and opportunities for their employees both in the workplace and outside the job. Sullivan was a member of the board of General Motors, and more than 130 companies of the 350 US subsidiaries in South Africa adopted the code. Many people, including me, saw the voluntary code as a way for businesses to keep operating while doing little to change the larger framework of apartheid. Critics like the African National Congress (ANC) called for full divestment from South Africa, while those supporting the Sullivan Principles argued divestment would only hurt the workers. As this debate evolved on Denison's campus, those of us supporting divestment had a real disadvantage in that Denison's president, Robert Good, knew more about African politics than we did. Good, who supported the Sullivan Principles, had been the US ambassador to Zambia and had a doctorate in international relations. We agreed to disagree on divestment, and the debate would follow me to Berkeley.

I also had the opportunity to write editorials in the newsletter of our Black Studies Center published, entitled *Alternative News*. Despite our small size, Denison was able to establish a diasporic perspective largely due to the presence of Naomi Garrett. Dr. Garrett, who was based at West Virginia State University, was one of the first in Black Studies to teach Caribbean literature. She had been invited by the English Department to speak at Denison and liked the campus enough to agree to become a visiting professor. I benefited personally by sitting in on some of her classes. It was through Naomi's contacts that we were able to invite French Guianese poet and politician Leon Damas, a co-founder of the Negritude Movement with Leopold Senghor and Aime Ceasar, to the 1977 NCBS conference at Ohio State. It was my privilege to serve as Damas's host during his visit.

Undoubtedly the highlight of my years at Denison was the adoption of our son, Charles Wesley, in 1978. Named for his two grandfathers, Wes was two months old when we brought him home from Catholic Social Services in Columbus, Ohio. Of course, the grandparents were thrilled to have another grandchild to spoil, and we built an addition to our little house in Granville.

Slightly over a year after Wesley's adoption, I came home from work one afternoon, and Loretta told me to have a seat. It's a good thing I did because she proceeded to announce that she was pregnant. Once we spread the news, a host of friends told us they knew couples who had adopted only to have produced a child of their own later. Nonetheless, we were happily surprised that the family would now number five.

Loretta and I had agreed that our stay at Denison would not be permanent. I still wanted to be at a research university and not spend all my time in administration and teaching. Toward that goal, I had a job interview at Harvard in the fall of 1978. The interview went well, and I asked the department chair, Eileen Southern, how much Harvard would offer. She quoted a figure less than I was making at Denison. Since Harvard rarely tenured junior faculty, I asked what incentive I would have to leave Denison. She said, "It's Harvard." I said, "Goodbye."

While I had not planned to stay at Denison, the political science department made it easier to leave. My contract had called for me to come up for tenure after three years at Denison. Tenure would have to be in political science since Black Studies was a program with no tenure lines. Political science, however, said Provost Brakeman had not informed them of this arrangement and refused to consider me for tenure. Since Brakeman was a past chair of political science, I found it difficult to believe they were not informed. The conflict escalated to the point at which I hired an attorney. President Good offered to create a tenure line in Black Studies, but I believed one tenure line in a program rather than a department was not feasible. Ultimately, I decided it was not worth the effort to sue given my desire to move anyway.

I applied for several fellowships in 1979 and interviewed for a position in African American Studies (AAS) at the University of California at Berkeley. During the interview process, I stayed at the men's faculty club. I remember noting that there was both a men's and women's faculty club and later learned that women had not been admitted to the men's club until the mid-sixties. Most of the members of the AAS department came to my talk on the development of the Metropolitan Applied Research Center under Kenneth Clark. At that time the department members included Reginald Jones (Psychology), William Banks (Psychology), Margaret Wilkerson (Theater), Barbara Christian (English), Erskine Peters (English), Al Rabateau (History), Michel Laguerre (Anthropology), Percy Hintzen (Political Economy), Roy Thomas (English), and Albert Johnson (Film). While on campus, I also met with two political scientists—Carlos Munoz in ethnic studies and Judy Gruber in political science. Both warned me that Berkeley's reputation for liberalism was overrated. The political science department had never had an African American political scientist on its faculty and would not until the 21st century. Carlos had no relationship with political science despite being one of the first Chicano political scientists. When I asked Judy about possibly having my Black politics courses cross-listed with the department, she was not optimistic, saying she had wanted to teach women's politics but was told it would have to be as an additional course rather than part of a regular teaching load. Given that context, when the dean of social science asked me if I was interested in a joint appointment with political science, I said no with the experience at Denison fresh in my mind.

Ultimately, I received two fellowship offers and a job offer from Berkeley. I declined a junior Fulbright award in Paris and accepted a National Endowment for the Humanities (NEH) Post-doctoral Fellowship in Black Studies at Atlanta University. Berkeley agreed to wait a year to allow me to complete the NEH post-doctorate. In July 1980, a very pregnant Loretta, Adia, Wes, and I drove our car to Atlanta, followed by my brother, Oren, and cousin, Larry, with our furniture in a U-Haul van.

We had barely settled into a townhouse in Eastpoint, GA, near the new Hartsfield International Airport when Laura Anne was born on August 24, the morning after our 14th wedding anniversary. Adia started first grade and quickly picked up a southern accent. Either Loretta or I would walk her to the nearby school since the frightening Atlanta child murders began around that time. I joined volunteers one Saturday sweeping a wooded area for bodies. Many who followed the case believe that the man who was finally caught and convicted, Wayne Williams, was responsible for some but not all 28 murders.

On a happier note, the NEH Fellowship experience was outstanding. Our host was Richard Long, an English professor and local institution. Richard seemed to know a lot about many disciplines and even more gossip. Our group of NEH Fellows met and/or heard lectures by Toni Cade Bambara, Sterling Brown, Romare Bearden, Benjamin Mays, and James Baldwin, among others. A highlight for me was having a drink with Baldwin. The fellowship was an opportunity to retrain myself in a new discipline that I had helped to start as a student.

Each one of our small groups of NEH Fellows had expertise that enriched our discussions. I played tennis with one fellow, and Loretta and I served as witnesses at his wedding in Atlanta. Another fellow taught community college in Berkeley, and I picked her brain about my future home. Another Californian, Frances Smith Foster, an English professor from San Diego State University, became a good friend. She and her two children lived in our development, which allowed us to share rides to the Atlanta campus and even take our children on a trip to Disney World together. Later Fran and I would co-author an article on Black Women's Studies.

Loretta and I enjoyed our time in Atlanta. She found time to do some work with the Southern Christian Leadership Conference's Joseph Lowry and his wife. We even drove out to Stone Mountain, Georgia, to see the monumental relief of Robert E. Lee carved into the rock. My father, who had proclaimed he would only go South if General Sherman went again, was probably turning over in his grave. It was with some reluctance, but also a great deal of excitement, that the five of us packed into our little Datsun without air-conditioning and set out for California in the summer of 1981.

5
From Black Studies to African diaspora to American cultures

Berkeley (CA) was a radical change from Denison. The student population was three times the size of Howard or Chicago and the entire Denison student body could fit in the campus auditorium. I liked that Berkeley, as a public institution, was vastly more affordable for low- and middle-income families than elite schools like Stanford. However, public funds came with state oversight. The university was proud of its host of Nobel Laureates and virtually any subject you could think of was taught or researched on campus. Still, the African American student population was less than five percent, and Black alums from the late 1960s said there were more international students than African American students when they arrived. The Black faculty numbered less than three percent of the academic senate (tenured and tenure track faculty) and would remain at roughly that level for most of my time there. In fact, about half the Black faculty on campus were in African American Studies (AAS).

Only a few of the AAS faculty had joint appointments with other departments, which meant the department had full control of its tenure lines and curriculum. Whether Black Studies was insti-tutionalized as a center, program, or department was influenced by several factors. Was the campus located in a large urban area or a small town? Was it an elite school with an upper-class pop-ulation of many legacy students or a public college with many first-generation, part-time, and commuter students? Was the campus ethnically and racially mixed or homogenous?

Taking all these factors into consideration, it is remarkable that Black student demands were relatively the same nationwide. Historian Nathan Huggins' 1982 report on the status of Black Studies summarized them as: 1. The political need for turf and a place, 2. The psychological need for identity, and 3. The academic need for recognition. Huggins and the Ford Foundation, which commissioned the report, favored an interdisciplinary program approach (Yale model). The model placed an emphasis on the third point, believing that by integrating the traditional disci-plines, Black Studies would automatically gain the legitimacy of those disciplines. Black students, on the other hand, almost uniformly desired departments giving priority to turf Blacks con-trolled, including community outreach and curriculum reflective of identity needs (nationalist model).

Black Studies at Cal started at roughly the same time as Denison in 1968; however, the forces surrounding its creation were far dif-ferent. A student-initiated course entitled "Social Analysis 139X" offered in the fall of 1968 by four faculty and one guest lecturer—Black Panther leader Eldridge Cleaver—lit the fuse. Immediately, Governor Ronald Reagan and Cleaver began trading insults, and FBI Director J. Edgar Hoover fed stakeholders inflammatory material. The university changed the rules governing lectures to one class per semester, sparking the occupation and vandalization of a campus building for sixteen hours. Ultimately, Cleaver delivered six lectures.

The intrusion of the administration and regents, not to mention the governor and FBI, served to build support for an autonomous department. Martin Luther King's assassination in April 1968 had already caused the Afro-American Studies Union (AASU) to submit a proposal for Black Studies. It opened by stating their alienation from the university and the irrelevance of a Berkeley degree to the communities they represented. It states:

"It is important to note here that our proposal is not a product of reaction. We are well beyond reaction. We are addressing ourselves to a basic change of attitude. This change is primarily a product of self-discovery. A kind of self-discovery that has snatched our minds from the rank of a historically insignificant, persecuted, minority and placed us among the world's majority to populace which is crying from one end of the earth to the other that 'we are'. We are decided that we alone can define ourselves, that we are beautiful despite the white negative concept of us, that we have a history, an art, and a culture that no race or nation can stamp out our 'souls' no matter the intensity of this foolish effort."

The proposal called for the appointment of a Black Studies coordinator whose primary duty would be establishing an Afro-American Studies Department modeled after one described by Nathan Hare in his "Conceptual Proposal for Black Studies". In addition, community outreach was a significant part of the demand, including provisions for experimental course development and course offerings through Berkeley's extension program.

Over the next year, Berkeley's small group of Black students and faculty would support the proposal while several prominent White faculty expressed their anger at not being consulted and promoted a center or interdisciplinary program citing the need for academic legitimacy. When the university rejected key elements of the proposal, including community outreach and departmental autonomy, the AASU, joined by other student activists organized as the Third World Liberation Front (TWLF), launched a student strike on January 22, 1969. Governor Reagan quickly mobilized the California National Guard, portraying the strike as a struggle between "primitives and the defenders of civilization". The TWLF responded by expanding the AASU demands to include an autonomous College of Third World or Ethnic Studies that would include four departments: Afro-American Studies, Chicano Studies, Asian Studies, and Native American Studies. This new college would also house an institute of race and community relations and an extension program. After two months of intense struggle, the university authorized the creation of an interim structure in the form of a Department of Ethnic Studies with four subfields reporting directly to the Chancellor. This temporary structure became permanent, and in 1972, Afro-American Studies split from Ethnic Studies to form a separate department within the College of Liberal Arts.

When I began teaching at Cal in the fall of 1981, it was soon clear to me that there was still some tension between the two departments and older students and faculty who believed AAS had been co-opted. Ethnic Studies reporting directly to the chancellor and AAS reporting to the dean of social sciences made it nearly impossible for faculty from the two departments to co-teach courses, as Carlos Munoz and I discovered when we tried to offer a joint course on social movements. We gave up the teaching proposal but did co-author an article on Black-Chicano coalitions. We believe it was the first publication co-authored by members of the two departments.

It also became clear to me that both departments lacked a key ingredient of any successful department at a research university—a graduate program. Graduate students usually taught large introductory courses and served as teaching assistants or research assistants. They not only freed faculty to teach courses directly related to their research but also did much of the tedious research work. For example, the well-known neoconservative political scientist Aaron Wildavsky and I had lunched a few times. At one such lunch, I asked him what research he was engaged in. Wildavsky said he was taking on the environmental movement. When I asked what aspect of the movement, he replied to all of it. He had four research assistants and was well funded. I had no research assistants and little funding (summer grants). Yet we were both judged by the same metrics when it came to promotions. Of course, the work graduate students did was regarded as paying dues for entering the profession. In short, faculty in the disciplines were training their replacements.

Three years after my arrival, in the fall of 1984, Asian American Studies professor Ron Takaki led a successful effort to establish the first comprehensive Ethnic Studies Ph.D. program in the United States. African American Studies joined Ethnic Studies in supporting the Ethnic Studies Graduate Group with the understanding that we were not foreclosing the possibility of a separate African American Studies doctoral program. Ron, aware that for more than a decade the two departments had engaged in few, if any, joint projects despite the rhetoric of the TWLF, asked me to chair the graduate group while he served as the graduate student advisor. Graduate students in the program would be required to study two of the four minority groups comprising our two departments and include methods courses from traditional disciplines. While the comparative framework was novel, students complained they were essentially doing twice the work of graduate students in the traditional departments. Moreover, the few Black students who entered the program expressed a desire to focus solely on the Black experience.

Our department had talked about a Ph.D. program for years, but the idea lacked momentum. The success of the Ethnic Studies Graduate Group spurred us to action. While serving as acting department chair in 1987–88, I met with the graduate dean to ask about the formal requirements. He said he had no idea since no doctoral programs had been established during his deanship. Fortunately, one of his senior staff did know the process, and we soon had a list of the obstacles to overcome.

There is a fine line to walk when starting a new discipline. First, the subject matter must be distinguishable from subjects already taught in existing disciplines. When, for example, political science was established in the early twentieth century, critics said the subject was already being covered in law schools and philosophy departments. And within the political science proponents themselves, there was division between those with a narrow focus on government and others with a broader perspective on political behavior. Even today there are a few departments of government instead of political science, even though the curriculums are basically the same. Once a proposed new discipline draws its boundaries, however, the subject matter can't be so different that it lacks coherence or credibility.

In a series of workshops, meetings, and retreats, AAS addressed all these issues and more. Of course, race as the focus of the discipline was new, but we also had to decide whether to limit our offerings to the United States or take a broader diasporian view, which might require additional faculty positions. To increase the chances of acceptance, Takaki had agreed to establish the Ethnic Studies doctorate with no new faculty. The direction of the program was not a foregone conclusion since the initial impetus of Black Studies had been to serve the local communities from which students came. However, there was an older tradition of intellectuals such as W. E. B. DuBois, Ralph Bunche, Paul Robeson, and others who had a global perspective on race. In addition, Berkeley's student body was witnessing a significant increase in students from Africa and the Caribbean. Ironically, this influx was occurring at the same time California was eliminating affirmative action at the local and state levels. Ultimately, the decision was made to include the African diaspora. Thanks to the hard work of Professors Margaret Wilkerson and Percy Hintzen, the department was the recipient of three successive Ford Foundation grants to assist in developing the graduate program. When the program was officially approved in the spring of 1996, it became the third Black Studies doctoral program in the country and the first with an African diaspora focus.

As the first graduate student advisor in the new program, I got the unenviable task of drafting the requirements to complete the M.A. and Ph.D. Many of our applicants were older than most programs because they said they had been waiting their whole lives for such an opportunity. As we had hoped, the students in the program brought new energy and ideas to the department.

Around the same time, we were laying the foundations for an AAS doctoral program; another battle over multiculturalism in the curriculum was brewing. Once again the issue was fueled by students. In 1988, Berkeley's freshman class was 40 percent White, 25 percent Asian, 17 percent Latino/a, and 12 percent Black. In short, the campus demographics were majority minority. In this context, Ron Takaki approached me during the

Ford Foundation- Black Studies Meeting - Nov. 30, 1987

Photo 12 Charles at the Ford Foundation meeting of leading Black Studies departments/programs (1987)

1986–1987 academic year about proposing an Ethnic Studies/ African American Studies graduate requirement for all Berkeley undergraduates. My first response was, what took Berkeley so long. We did something similar at Denison a decade ago! My next response was to join Ron and student representative Mark Min on a Faculty/Student Steering Committee for an Ethnic Studies graduation requirement. Chancellor Ira Michael Heyman and Provost Rod Park sought to get in front of the issue by appointing their own ad hoc committee on education and ethnicity led by White anthropologist Bill Simmons that would examine the possibilities of a "cultural pluralism" requirement. By the fall of 1987, there were at least three proposals being discussed. The Faculty/Student Committee favored a "Peoples Plan" that required students to choose a course from existing courses in AAS and ES. Provost Park was absolutely opposed to this proposal and put forth his own plan asking each of the departments in social science (excluding psychology) to develop one or two courses that satisfied the requirement. Park's plan would avoid a debate by simply attaching the ethnicity requirement to the existing American History and Institution requirement already in place. The Ad Hoc Committee developed a proposal that would require Academic Senate approval. They initially looked at about 50 existing courses that examined racial minorities but were concerned that courses on one minority group might be too narrow and exclude Europeans.

In March 1988, the Chair of Ethnic Studies, Alex Saragoza, and I met with the Ad Hoc Committee to work out a joint proposal. We had the support of 70 faculty who signaled their support for a cultural diversity requirement as well as the support of many key student organizations, including the student government. What emerged from the Ad Hoc Committee after a series of workshops, boycotts, and public forums was a "cultural pluralism requirement of one or more for the following four minorities: Afro-Americans, Asian Americans, Chicano/Latino Americans, and Native Americans. Many of the objections raised were ones I had heard ten years earlier from the Denison faculty. By the time the proposal was voted on in May 1988, it was renamed the "American Cultures" requirement, and courses had to give in-depth coverage to at least two of the four minority groups. In addition, the proposal now included a Center for the Study of American Cultures to support faculty and graduate students in developing courses. This latter addition was important in gaining my support. Over the course of the year, I had been asked to join the Ad Hoc Committee as a replacement for a member who was in poor health. While I thought the comparative perspective could be instructive, I doubted whether enough faculty were trained to do it. The Center gave me some confidence that with support and training, there were enough Cal faculty to pull it off. In fact, the proposal would eventually call for the examination of three groups. Moreover, European Americans were added as a group. Instead of being viewed as the dominant culture, they would now be decentered as one of several "minority" groups. Finally, the proposal opened the teaching of courses for the requirement to all departments, not just Ethnic Studies or social sciences. This opening would lead to some very creative course offerings from such places as the School of Engineering, the School of Architecture, and the College of Natural Resources, among others.

After a great deal of debate, including rallies at the state capital (I went to Sacramento at least twice to lobby), the requirement passed the academic senate in April 1989 with 227 faculty in favor and 194 against. I, along with AAS department colleagues William Banks and Barbara Christian, was a part of the first summer class of "American Cultures Fellows" who came together to develop new courses to meet the requirement. Although I initially proposed a course on "Ethnic and Racial Succession in Urban Politics," I began to think that a course on minorities and human rights might offer something not available in the curriculum and coincide with the human rights work I was doing off campus. I eventually taught a course on "Human Rights and US Foreign Policy" that examined the influence of three racial/ethnic groups on human rights policy. The first time I offered the course, it included African Americans, Japanese Americans, and Native Americans. The second time it was offered, the three groups were African Americans, Irish Americans, and Native Americans. I learned something every time I taught the course.

Establishing a graduate program that enabled AAS faculty to pursue research and replicate themselves in the form of future scholars and professors was important, although not all our graduates pursued careers in academia. Equally passing a general education requirement, making our history and culture a part of the educational experience for all students, was also important. However, these advances had come after years of struggle with generations of students leading the way. What remained to be done was to secure a place at the table. To be in the room where decisions were made rather than out in the street looking in. Toward that end, I joined the university administration.

Bill Simmons, dean of social sciences and the former head of the Ad Hoc Committee on Education and Ethnicity, saw me in the parking lot one day and asked if I would be interested in taking on the new position of faculty equity associate. This curiously titled new position was the result of combining two formerly half-time positions—the faculty affirmative action assistant for race and the faculty affirmative action assistant for gender. The new full-time position would essentially be the faculty affirmative action officer or what is now called DEI officer. Since California voters had recently passed Proposition 209, eliminating affirmative action in local and state public employment, public education, and public contracting, I felt I should do all I could to stop the door of opportunity from closing at Berkeley. I accepted the position to begin in the fall 1997 academic year.

My office was a corner suite in California Hall near Chancellor Robert Berdahl's office. I had a secretary but no staff (later I would be bumped downstairs by an incoming vice-chancellor). My major duty was to review all hires, promotions, and terminations for bias. Only the chancellor, vice-chancellor/provost, vice-provost, and I had complete access to all personnel files. Additional duties included running faculty workshops, often with the vice chancellor/provost, on best hiring practices, meeting with deans and department chairs, reviewing the campus affirmative action plan, and hearing grievances from faculty who believed they had been discriminated against. Perhaps my biggest surprise was the vast disparity in salaries between departments and schools. Among social science departments, for example, economics department faculty were on a different and higher scale than other social science departments. Another example was the business school, which paid a newly minted doctorate in budgeting more than a renowned senior sociologist up for promotion in his department. There was also consistent gender bias in salaries that required multiple efforts to correct.

Despite my access to case files and being able to intervene to reverse tenure decisions in a few cases, I was not a member of the chancellor's cabinet. Chancellor Berdahl was opposed to a vice chancellor for affirmative action or equity, believing concentrating responsibility in one position would let departments off the hook. I, on the other hand, thought we needed an advocate at the most senior level and someone who would keep the pressure on in a decentralized system. To advance this discussion, I convinced Berdahl to convene a task force to examine the issue of implementing DEI on campus. He appointed the dean of the graduate school for public policy, Michael Nacht, as chair of the task force, and I served to staff it. At the end of a year of deliberations, the task force recommended a cabinet-level position for affirmative action. In the meantime, my title was changed to associate vice-provost, and I participated in cabinet meetings the last year of my administrative term.

Sometimes being an insider was uncomfortable. I was told of a secret passage in California Hall that would let the chancellor and other senior administrators escape if the building was occupied. That knowledge was almost put to the test when Ethnic Studies faculty and students, joined by supporters, protested in front of the building in the spring of 1999. What came to be called the Ethnic Studies student strike spawned a 24-hour vigil that the students said would continue until their demands for more recourses were met. I was called to a late-night meeting at the chancellor's residence to decide whether police should be called in to clear the protesters out. I advocated against such action (to no avail). At the same time I was listening to the chancellor's plans, I was invited to a meeting of protesters, many of whom I knew as they devised strategy. We were able to arrange a meeting between Berdahl and the protesters, which I staffed, that led to an agreement. Among the demands met was the establishment of an institute on race research, which was a part of the original TWLF demands. The chancellor agreed to fund an institute that was not yet in existence. I was given the task of chairing the committee that drafted the plans for what became the Center for Race and Gender. My greatest fear as chair was that radical students on the committee would sink any plan that deviated from their initial demands. Instead, the most difficult committee member was a sociology professor who seemed to object to everything. My second task was to find an acceptable director for the center. This became problematic when the only faculty member to volunteer was a White male professor of natural resources. Disaster was averted when I was able to convince a female Asian Studies professor who researched labor issues among Asian domestic workers to take the position. By my third year in this position, I was also serving as AAS department chair even though I was full-time in the chancellor's administration. I felt I had done all I could to institutionalize DEI and moved back to the AAS department. The following year, a new chancellor, Robert Birgeneau, named a vice chancellor for equity and inclusion. Although I had nothing to do with the title, Birgeneau was fond of repeating a distinction I made to him between diversity and affirmative action. I said hiring a middle-class Argentinian English professor might enhance diversity, but it was not affirmative action. Hiring a Chicano English professor from a working-class family in Oakland would be affirmative action. In that sense, diversity replaces affirmative action.

Proposition 209 had severely impacted the number of underrepresented students on campus. By fall 2003, for example, Blacks in the freshman class had declined to less than one hundred, with only one-third African American men. I chaired a search committee for the director of undergraduate admissions, and we eventually chose Berkeley's first Black director of admissions. I was also on the search committee that hired john a. powell to develop what became the Center for Otherness and Belonging. Among the endless meetings of these committees and others like the Peace and Conflict Studies program and the new Human Rights Center, some were intensely emotional and others intensely boring. I remember as a junior faculty member on the review committee for the graduate school of public policy finding it hard to believe that the eight tenured White males on the faculty were doing all they could for affirmative action when several had published books and articles opposing it. On another occasion, I was shocked when two professors in Peace and Conflict Studies narrowly averted coming to blows over a minor issue. I always told students in awe of any professor to observe them at a faculty meeting as they battled over parking spaces. It turns out you need to win a Nobel prize in your field to receive a dedicated space—unfair for those of us in fields that don't compete for the Nobel prize!

6
Office hours

Every faculty member at Berkeley is supposed to post their office hours on their door. Generally, you should have one hour of office duty for every three hours in class, although this rule is seldom enforced. At the University of Chicago, where I went to graduate school, it was rumored that one professor—who shall remain nameless—would come into his office, open the door, hang up his coat, and then leave for the rest of the day. I thought such actions short-changed the students and missed an opportunity to know them better.

At Berkeley, you never knew who would walk through your door. It was often students who wanted to argue about a grade—not my favorite kind of visit but a teachable moment, nonetheless. And I am delighted that I no longer must grade papers now that artificial intelligence may or may not have played a part in their composition.

Another type of visitor was students seeking a letter of recommendation. Sometimes this occurred with students I barely knew, but they had often been in courses with teaching assistants rather than professors. Once when I asked Professor Harry Edwards if he knew the names of all his students, he said he barely knew the names of his teaching assistants—he had 26 of them. One of my favorites, Ronnie Stevenson (a former Black

Panther Party (BPP) member), took all six undergraduate courses I taught and frequently came to office hours. Ronnie joined the Party as a high school student in Berkeley and can be seen in the background of the documentaries on the Panthers. His parents had been members of the Communist Party USA a generation earlier. Ronnie had been falsely accused of participating in a murder and had gone underground, worked, and become a union leader in a Ford factory in New Jersey for several years. When he returned to Berkeley after some legal assistance, he was able to resume his education at UC Berkeley. Ronnie had developed a negative view of many Panther activities.

The Black Panther Party had changed dramatically from the organization Ronnie had joined in the late 1960s. From its founding in Oakland in the fall of 1966 by Bobby Seale and Huey Newton to its armed lobbying of the California State Legislature on May 2, 1967, the party had steady local growth based on its mission to police the police. However, when 30 armed Panthers arrived at the state capitol in Sacramento to lobby against the Mulford Act, which proposed to outlaw the carrying of loaded firearms in public, the effect was instantaneous. Newton had studied the existing gun laws closely and knew the Panthers were within their rights to carry the weapons openly. The police, however, arrested them for disrupting the legislative session rather than breaking the gun law. The resulting publicity made the Panthers famous overnight. Within a few months, Newton had declared the Black Panther Party for Self-Defense a vanguard party, and the new *Black Panther* newspaper published a ten-point program (list of demands). The demands were a mix of both revolutionary and reformist goals. The former included an exemption from military service for all Black men, the freeing of all Black men held in jails, an end to the robbery by Whites of the Black community, and self-determination. Among the more reformist demands were full employment, Black Studies, decent housing, fair trials, and an end to police brutality. As a vanguard party, the BPP believed in an "armed revolution, a permanent revolution, the creation of as many Viet Nams as are necessary to defeat US racism and imperialism throughout the world (Newton, Essays, n.d. p. 1)". Although several of these demands were similar to those of the Revolutionary Action Movement (RAM), Newton decided to wage his war above ground rather than underground like RAM. Moreover, the mix of revolutionary and reformist goals made it possible to form allies across a broad range of activist groups.

Both high school and university students in Berkeley were members or supporters of the Panthers, who actively recruited on campuses. As the party became a national organization in the fall of 1968, it became difficult for the Central Committee based in Oakland to control the rapid growth. Members joined who used the Party as a cover for a variety of illegal activities, from robbing service stations and taverns to murder. The party began publishing ten rules of behavior in each issue of the *Black Panther*, and that list quickly expanded to 26 rules prohibiting many activities. By January 1969, Seale froze membership at the 45 existing chapters. With Huey Newton in jail in 1967 and Eldridge Cleaver (Minister of Information) in exile, Bobby Seale began the Black Panther community programs.

As a former government poverty program employee, Seale had always been interested in social services. Beginning with the first Breakfast for Children Program in Oakland in September 1968, Panther programs rapidly expanded to include food distribution, free clothing, liberation schools, housing cooperatives, transportation for prison visits, and pest control, among other programs. In fact, it was the free breakfast program that first involved Ronnie with the Panthers. While these programs were widely applauded, they marked a significant change in political direction from that envisioned by Newton and Cleaver.

By the time Ronnie returned from the East Coast, the Black Panthers were, for all intents and purposes, dead as an organization. The party had been split apart internally and externally, lost allies, and been repressed. Opponents of the war in Vietnam had been the Panthers' most prominent ally in the late 1960s. But as the war wound down and the draft was ended, that source of support dried up. Many activists from the civil rights movement, especially those in direct action organizations like SNCC and CORE, shifted their activities to the electoral arena. The National Black Political Assembly in 1972 symbolized this shift to electoral politics as Black Nationalists and civil rights activists joined forces—briefly. From 1969 to 1975, the number of Black elected officials tripled. In 1972, Bobby Seale ran for mayor of Oakland, and Elaine Brown ran for the city council. Those activists who went the other direction and espoused revolutionary action were also the main targets of COINTEL and were either jailed, exiled, or killed. The assassination of Illinois Panther leaders Fred Hampton and Mark Clark in December 1969 in Chicago is a prime example of the federal government working with state and local officials to eliminate Panther leadership. Finally, revolutionary governments that had welcomed radical Panther leadership and encouraged international solidarity began to move toward some accommodation with the United States government.

During his time away from Berkeley, Ronnie had been drawn away from Newton's "revolutionary suicide" and toward the "redemptive suffering" of Martin Luther King. He harassed me so much about teaching a course on Martin Luther King that I gave in and put one together. It turned out to be my favorite and most popular course. In relatively short order, Ronnie organized a group named the MLK Convocation Day Committee that had the student union renamed after King, had a major street renamed in King's honor, held a major convocation honoring King every year, participated in the South African divestment movement, and established a tutoring program in local Berkeley schools called Break-the-Cycle. I remember attending a Berkeley City Council meeting once to support Ronnie's request for city funding for the tutoring program. As the meeting dragged on for hours, I remember thinking there is such a thing as too much democracy!

Another visitor to my office had undergone a radical change in direction. A community member who audited my classes on occasion and supported himself selling T-shirts brought Eldridge Cleaver in to meet me in October 1991. Cleaver had joined the Panthers soon after being paroled in 1966. He had been in and out of prison for a variety of offenses ranging from marijuana use to robbery for most of his young life. In prison, however, he had read widely and learned how to write. By the time of his release, he had established a relationship with *Ramparts* magazine and was working on the manuscript for *Soul on Ice*. He was at the Panthers protest in Sacramento as a reporter for *Ramparts* but soon joined the Panthers as Minister of Communication. Newton had a high-pitched voice and hated public speaking, while Seale was more interested in organizing than public speaking. This left Cleaver as the major spokesperson for the organization and the editor of the popular *Black Panther* newspaper.

The publication of *Soul on Ice* in 1968 made Cleaver a major spokesperson for the radical left. The book was widely read on college campuses and became a best seller nationally and internationally. Seale's book *Seize the Time* was not published until 1970, and Newton's *Revolutionary Suicide* came out two years later. That left college students in the late 1960s like me dependent on Cleaver for an inside view of what the Panthers were about. But *Soul on Ice* was much more than an insider view of the Panthers. Like Malcolm X's autobiography, it was a story of Cleaver's self-redemption. In fact, Cleaver states, "I have, so to speak, washed my hands in the blood of the martyr, Malcolm X, whose retreat from the precipice of madness created new room for others to turn about in, and I am now caught up in that tiny space, attempting a maneuver of my own" (p. 66). He rejected the teachings of Elijah Muhammad as well as "Negro leaders" with a "hat-in-hand" approach to revolution. Cleaver saw the rebellion of college students at places like Berkeley as the catalyst for "the brewing revolt of the whites". And, of course, the Panthers were the vanguard, leading the way.

On April 6, 1968, two days after the assassination of Martin Luther King, Jr., Cleaver was involved in a shoot-out with Oakland police that killed seventeen-year-old Bobby Hutton and led to Cleaver's exile. Cleaver had been on the presidential ballot in 1968 as the candidate on the Peace and Freedom Party ticket. However, first from Cuba and later Algeria, Cleaver increasingly took a revolutionary line, calling for the training of guerillas and criticizing the move to local politics by Seale. With Newton in jail and later hooked on crack, this rupture would lead to the demise of the organization.

By the time Cleaver visited me in 1991, he had undergone another transformation. Having worked out some arrangement with United States authorities, he returned to the country in 1975 as a member of Rev. Moon's Unification Church. He would later join the Church of Latter-Day Saints and become an active supporter of the conservative wing of the Republican Party, divorcing Kathleen Cleaver in 1987. Cleaver's various business ventures had not gone well, and by 1991 he was collecting trash for recycling. His interest in visiting me concerned selling his papers for cash. After a chat recalling some of his earlier activities, I told him I would make a pitch to the librarian for purchasing the papers. Cleaver graciously signed my old college copy of *Soul on Ice*, saying I didn't look old enough to remember the 1960s. I thought to myself, my life has not gone through as many transformations as yours! He ended up selling the papers to Stanford University.

I met another Panther leader from the revolutionary wing of the Party at San Quentin. When I arrived at Berkeley, some faculty were participating in a program at the famous prison called Self-Advancement Through Education (SATE). It involved giving some lectures at San Quentin in a program coordinated by the inmates. I soon volunteered to give lectures on Black history/politics and one day found myself in the visitor's room with the coordinator of the program. I was told he was in prison for the murder of three people in a Los Angeles drug deal gone bad. He was built like a linebacker and carefully explained to me that going near White or Latino prisoners could be dangerous. He clearly had my attention.

My first lecture drew a decent crowd, and among them was Geronimo Pratt (aka Geronimo Ji-Jaga), a BPP leader from Los Angeles. Although Pratt was a heavily decorated Vietnam veteran, he had been jailed 37 times as well as beaten and shot by the police because of his Party activity. In the fall of 1970, he was charged and in 1972 convicted of the murder of Caroline Olson in a flawed trial that was criticized by Amnesty International, among others. When I met him in the early 1980s, he was one of the longest-serving Panther prisoners. Early in my lecture, he asked what Blacks should call themselves. I said my preferred term was African American because it indicated a place of origin and current location. He countered that we were not nor ever had been American. We should call ourselves the "new African people". I said you are free to use any terminology you like, and we continued with the lecture. Pratt would serve 27 years in prison, eight of them in solitary confinement. Finally, in 1997, his sentence was vacated, and he moved to Tanzania. In the brief time I was at San Quentin, I encountered several young Black men who would not have been out of place on Berkeley's campus. In fact, the university now has an "underground scholars" program for students who have been incarcerated. Unfortunately, the SATE program ended after I gave only a few lectures. I was waiting at the entrance to the prison one day to be cleared when I heard shots. I was told there was a disturbance, and the prison went into lock-down and stayed there for months. A Black guard told me it was not uncommon for guards to plant weapons with a prison gang with the expectation that a conflict would occur and the prison would lock down, ensuring the guards increased over time. By the time this lockdown ended, the coordinators of SATE had been transferred to other prisons, and the program died.

Occasionally interesting visiting faculty and graduate students would stop by and introduce themselves. One graduate student from Tunisia came by to ask Roy Thomas (an AAS colleague) and me to meet Rached Ghannouchi, the head of the Movement of Islamic Tendency, which would later become the Ennahda Party in his country. We agreed to meet him for dinner in San Francisco. I distinctly remember him chewing out the owner of the Tunisian restaurant we dined at for serving alcohol. He invited Roy and me to join him on an all-expenses-paid trip to Mecca. Not only did I think this was a bad idea for a non-Muslim but also bad given my leadership in Amnesty International at the time. Ghannouchi became a key figure in the Arab Spring movement.

My favorite visitors, however, were non-students. A few came by when I was chair of AIUSA to ask me to have the organization take up their human rights cases. On one memorable occasion, a woman came in to complain that devices had been implanted in her body by either aliens or the government and she was being tracked at all times. In such cases, I usually said I had to go to a meeting or class and headed for the door.

Other visitors stopped by because I was a political scientist and they wanted to talk politics. One such person was John Connolly. John had developed the idea of a non-partisan print debate before elections that would allow for a thorough discussion of relevant issues. He couldn't get anyone in the political science department interested, so he came to me. Although I pointed out some of the obstacles to his project, John was persistent and managed to get several newspapers to publish his idea as an opinion piece or letter to the editor as well as several representatives to endorse the idea. John pushed the idea through several election cycles, and we became good friends in the interim.

It turned out that John was a world-class sailor who taught ocean sailing across the globe. He even had a knot named after him and had patented a life-saving technique for people falling overboard. John lived in Sausalito and occasionally took my wife and me sailing on the Bay and, in one memorable trip, Tahiti. John owned the Modern Sailing Academy in Sausalito until his untimely death several years ago.

Another memorable office visitor was a retired Harvard alumna, who came to see me because I taught African American Studies. Rather, he came to see me because he opposed much of what we taught on the subject. While African American Studies at Berkeley could not be considered Afrocentric in a narrow sense, it did support a broad range of approaches and methods in researching the African diaspora. In 1980, Molefi Asante had published *Afrocentricity*, a book in which he attacked the Eurocentrism of much of the research done on African Americans and called for an African-centered research methodology. Asante was heavily influenced by Maulana Karenga's 1960 work on *Kawaida* Theory and the African scholar Cheikh Anta Diop. His work was influential enough that he was able to establish the first doctoral program in Black Studies at Temple University in 1986 (U. Mass. at Amherst would est. the second and Berkeley the third). It was not until his third book, *Kemet, Afrocentricity, and Knowledge*, that Asante turned his focus to ancient Egypt (Kemet). However, it was with Martin Bernal's 1987 book (3 vol.), *Black Athena: The Afroasiatic Roots of Classical Civilization*, that the culture wars were fully joined.

Was Cleopatra Black? This question was the one that seemed to enrage opponents of Afrocentrism. Perhaps Mary Lefkowitz's *Not Out of Africa* is the most comprehensive and emotional response to Bernal's work. The fact that Cleopatra ruled Egypt a thousand years after the pyramids were built or that modern racial categories had no meaning in ancient Egypt seemed to matter little. The debate often ignored the larger question raised by Asante and especially Bernal about the influence of Egypt on the ancient Greeks. Bernal argues that this influence was acknowledged by the Greeks but had been erased by racist European scholars in the eighteenth and nineteenth centuries. Trained as a scholar of Chinese history and language, Bernal had switched his focus to Egypt in 1975. He visited Berkeley for a lecture a year or two after the publication of *Black Athena* and was generally well-received. The belief that Western civilization's foundation rested in Greece was amplified by Alan Bloom's *The Closing of the American Mind* in 1987, the year Bernal's work was published. Thus, classics scholars and historians saw *Black Athena* as an attack on Western civilization itself. Egyptocentrism and Afrocentrism are related but not the same thing. According to

Wilson Moses, "Egyptocentrism is the sometimes sentimental, at other times cynical, attempt to claim ancient Egyptian ancestry for Black Americans. Afrocentrism, on the other hand, is simply the belief that the African ancestry of Black peoples, regardless of where they live, is an inescapable element of their various identities—imposed from within or without their own communities (Moses, 1998, p. 6)."

My office visitor especially took issue with claims that the Egyptians were African or that any Black civilization could have built Great Zimbabwe. I could usually count on at least one visit per semester to debate something he had read. Although I am not an Egyptologist, I found St. Claire Drake's work *Black Folk Here and There* the best treatment of this issue. At one of our last meetings, my visitor gave me a copy of the unpublished half-encyclopedia he had compiled. I confess I haven't read it, but its huge size makes an excellent doorstop.

Although he did not come to my office, another controversial visitor to Berkeley was cultural nationalist Maulana Karenga. Originally trained in political science and later social ethics, Karenga established the US organization in 1965 and created the African American holiday Kwanzaa the following year. His organization became bitter rivals of the Black Panthers in Los Angeles, leading to a deadly encounter at UCLA in 1969. I first heard Karenga speak at the national convention of the Congress of Racial Equality (CORE) in 1968 in Columbus, Ohio. He was on a program with Muhammad Ali and Floyd McKissick and was flanked by impressive-looking bodyguards. Karenga believed that "Christianity is a white religion. It has a white God, and any

'Negro' who believes in it is a sick 'Negro'. How can you pray to a white man? If you believe in him, no wonder you catch so much hell (Karenga, 1967, p. 25)." Obviously, the US leader was no fan of Martin Luther King. He says the "[o]nly thing non-violence proved was how savage whites were (p. 13)". Like the Panther leadership, Karenga also spent time in prison in the 1970s. By the 1980s, he had learned hieroglyphics and published a version of the Egyptian Book of the Dead. While Karenga did not come by my office, he and his wife, Tiamoyo, did come by my home to meet my family. Later I would write a letter of recommendation for him for a position in Black Studies at California State University in Long Beach. Like Ronnie Stevenson, Karenga also changed his position on King. His Pan African Institute honors King every January 15th. On occasion, I thought I might try to get Karenga and some of the Bay Area Panthers together at Berkeley for a discussion of the 1960s but ultimately decided it might not go well.

Another visitor to Berkeley I got to know was the Marxist historian, Herbert Aptheker. Aptheker taught a course on racism and the law at Berkeley's law school for several years. The African American Studies department was fortunate to have him lecture on W. E. B. DuBois. Aptheker was a close friend of DuBois and his literary executor. Although well-known for his expertise in African American history, Aptheker's affiliation with the Communist Party kept him from teaching in any American university from 1939 to 1969. Over the course of several dinners, I enjoyed listening to his stories of personal experiences with DuBois, Carter Woodson, E. Franklin Frazier, and others. I was almost ashamed when such a distinguished scholar as Aptheker asked me to write a letter of recommendation for a position at Santa Clara University. He was briefly employed there before a trustee discovered his name on an office door and had his position terminated. So much for academic freedom!

7
Witnessing Black political history: Gary, San Francisco, and Chicago

Physically, Gary, Indiana, is not an attractive city. Now known as the hometown of Michael Jackson and his family, for many years it was the home of the United States Steel Corporation. Residents of Gary paid a price for jobs at the steel mill as the city was permanently encased in smog. By the time of the National Black Political Convention (NBPC) from March 10–12, 1972, most of the jobs had disappeared and the city was in decline.

It was chosen as the site of the convention because Mayor Richard Hatcher had opened the city and its high school to this historic conference. Hatcher, along with Carl Stokes of Cleveland, had become the first African American mayors of major United States cities in 1967. The optimism surrounding the election of Black officials across the country, including the establishment of the Congressional Black Caucus (CBC) in 1970, had dimmed in the face of urban violence, assassinations, and the election of Richard Nixon. Four years after Nixon's "law and order" administration had dramatically increased the militarization of police departments across the country, and at the same time, reduced social welfare and social services, ending the war on poverty; it seemed that poverty had won. Moreover, Nixon's 1968 promise to quickly end the war in Vietnam remained unfulfilled.

These factors led Black leaders from the civil rights movement, the Black nationalist movement, and Black elected officials to call for the historic meeting. Yet while the convention was historic in its scope, it was not the first national Black political convention. Beginning in the 1830s and continuing into the 1850s, several National Negro Conventions were held. Led by such figures as Martin Delany, Henry Highland Garnet, and Frederick Douglass, delegates focused on such issues as abolition, colonization, voluntary emigration, and the status of free Blacks. In the twentieth century, Marcus Garvey's United Negro Improvement Association (UNIA) held large conventions filling Madison Square Garden in the 1920s. Nearly two decades later, the leftist National Negro Congress held national conferences focused on the New Deal with strong labor participation.

The NBPC, or Gary Convention, was co-chaired by CBC Chair Charles Diggs, Black nationalist poet and playwright Amiri Baraka, and Hatcher. Although Diggs and Hatcher were Democrats, the Gary Declaration issued by the convention made clear the dissatisfaction with both major parties. There were over 3,000 delegates and 5,000 observers at the meeting. The delegates were broadly representative of the national Black community and had been chosen in state conventions. Some were dominated by nationalists while others were led by Black elected officials and civil rights activists. I was an observer attached to the Illinois delegation led by Jesse Jackson. As a graduate student at the University of Chicago, I had worked on anti-machine politics with State Senator Richard Newhouse and attended political workshops of the Southern Christian Leadership Conference's (SCLC) Operation Breadbasket run by Calvin Morris and Leon Davis. That political work, as well as being a graduate student in political science, gave me access.

Three primary objectives were before the convention. First, the delegates had to decide whether to support one of the major party candidates in the upcoming presidential election or one of the unannounced Black leaders considering a run. The convention decided not to take a position on presidential candidates, although Congresswoman Shirley Chisholm would later announce her candidacy.

The second objective was the creation of a Black political party. Although Jackson and Ron Daniels of the Ohio delegation pushed for a separate party, the convention decided to give the major party candidates one last chance to respond to Black demands while the grassroots built a base for a Black party.

Finally, after a great deal of debate, the convention approved a Black Agenda that would be presented to the major party presidential candidates for their endorsement. The Black Agenda was a combination of both reformist and more radical policies. For example, reform objectives included environmental goals such as banning DDT, establishing a land bank for southern Black farmers, ending the death penalty, and ensuring a guaranteed annual income. More radical goals included ending sanctions on Cuba and implementing sanctions on South Africa. Ultimately, however, two issues were too much for the moderate forces at the convention to endorse. On the domestic front, Black nationalists succeeded in passing a demand to end forced school integration and especially busing. Leaders of groups like the NAACP and many elected officials opposed this agenda item. In foreign affairs, the convention opposed Israeli occupation of Palestine and supported self-determination for Palestinians over the opposition of these same delegates. Shortly after the Black Agenda was released, the CBC broke with the convention by issuing its own agenda, which supported busing and Israel. Although Democratic presidential candidate George McGovern would eventually endorse many of the reformist goals coming out of Gary, Chisholm launched her own presidential campaign (Chisholm, 1973). Chisholm's campaign attracted minimal support from women and Blacks, and McGovern would lose overwhelmingly to incumbent Richard Nixon.

The NBPC restructured itself as the National Black Political Assembly (NBPA) and met in Little Rock, Arkansas, in 1974. Hatcher and Atlanta Mayor Maynard Jackson participated, but the meeting was dominated by Black nationalists. By the time of the third meeting of the NBPA in Cincinnati in 1976, most of the Black elected officials had withdrawn from the group. The NBPA had hoped to run Congressman Ron Dellums on a third-party ticket for president, but he ultimately decided not to run. Ironically, at the last minute, the group endorsed Arizona Congressman Mo Udall for the Democratic nomination. It was not until the fourth NBPA convention in New Orleans in 1980 that an independent Black third party would be formed, the National Black Independent Political Party (NBIPP).

Third parties in the United States have generally assumed two forms—protest parties or ideological parties. Protest parties tend to arise when the two major parties ignore an issue that a significant number of voters feel strongly about, such as abolition, immigration, alcohol, taxes, and political corruption. Historical examples include the Free-Soil Party, Liberty Party, Populist Party, Know-Nothing Party, Progressive Party, Green Party, Tea Party, and the American Independent Party. These parties seldom last more than one or two election cycles since one of the major parties will co-opt their issue if it proves popular to voters. Ideological parties, on the other hand, are long-lived. Their voters are outside the mainstream, and their ideology is applied to a wide scope of issues ranging from minimal state to maximum state involvement. Such parties include the Libertarian Party, Communist Party, Socialist Party, and the American Nazi Party. The major parties generally avoid any attempt to attract these voters, assuming they would lose as many or more of their base by adopting extreme positions. The process for getting on the ballot is unique to each state, and it is difficult at best for their parties to launch national campaigns. A party like NBIPP is relatively rare in that it has a position over a range of issues but considers racial impact rather than ideology as criteria for support. The Green Party might be the nearest equivalent.

School integration and Israel would continue to divide Black voters throughout the 1970s, and obviously, support for Israel remains a contentious issue in the Black community. Full employment had widespread support in the Black community, including the CBC, and was passed in the form of the Humphrey-Hawkins Full Employment and Balanced Growth Act in 1976 but severely weakened by the Carter administration. It was not until Jesse Jackson's 1984 presidential bid that nationalist and liberal forces would come together again.

With the assassination of Martin Luther King, Jr., in 1968, there was no clear leader of the civil rights movement. However, with the election of Hatcher and Stokes in 1967 and the formation of the CBC in 1970, Black elected officials soon filled the leadership gap. In Newark, New Jersey, in 1970, Amiri Baraka provided crucial support for Kenneth Gibson's election. Even Black Panther Party leader Bobby Seale would run for mayor of Oakland in 1972. Seale was defeated, but Oakland soon had a Black mayor when Lionel Wilson was elected with Panther support in 1977.

Several civil rights leaders would also turn to electoral politics in the 1970s. Former Student Nonviolent Coordinating Committee (SNCC) leader Marion Barry became mayor of Washington, DC in 1979. Former King Aide Andrew Young would represent Atlanta in Congress from 1972 to 1976 and then join the Carter administration as ambassador to the United Nations. Young resigned in 1979 over a dispute involving relations with Israel. Former SNCC leader John Lewis was elected to Congress in 1987 and SNCC's Eleanor Holmes Norton in 1991.

Although Jesse Jackson had tested the mayoral waters in Chicago in 1972, he did not formally enter the electoral arena until his bid for the Democratic presidential nomination in 1984. The institutionalization of the civil rights movement flowed naturally from its emphasis on voting rights. Bayard Rustin, for example, had urged King to abandon his plans for the Poor People's Campaign to focus on voter registration, and foundations were much more willing to sponsor voting drives than protests. Thus, power shifted from litigation and the streets to city councils, state legislatures, and Congress. Traditional civil rights organizations like the NAACP and Urban League survived this shift, but the newer direct-action organizations like SNCC, the Congress of Racial Equality (CORE), and SCLC did not. Jimmy Carter's election with the help of Martin Luther King, Sr., initially renewed hope that electoral politics could advance Black equality. Carter's administration, however, was ultimately viewed as disappointing among Black voters. And, with the rise of Ronald Reagan, there were renewed cries to counter the rightward direction of American politics.

Jackson had been more successful than most of his Southern contemporaries in appealing to the young Black power advocates in the North. In Chicago, my wife and I often attended the Saturday morning meeting of SCLC's Operation Breadbasket (Jackson would later break from SCLC to form Operation People United to Serve Humanity—PUSH) in a theater on Chicago's South Side. In his mid-twenties, Jackson sported an Afro, bell-bottom trousers, and a large medallion rather than the Southern preachers' dark suit and close-cropped hair. He preached a message of economic empowerment and created a Black (business) expo urging his audience to buy Black and boycott stores not stocking Black products. We saw "little" Stevie Wonder perform at one of the first Black Expos. By holding Saturday meetings, Jackson was careful not to encroach on the Sunday morning gatherings of

Black churches. He had the good sense to surround his political sermons or jeremiads with an outstanding choir. Every meeting opened with Jackson leading the audience with the following invocation:

> *I am somebody,*
> *I may be poor,*
> *I may be uneducated,*
> *I may be unskilled,*
>   *but I am somebody.*
> *I may be prematurely pregnant,*
> *I may be on drugs,*
> *I may be victimized by racism,*
>   *but I am somebody.*
> *Respect me, Protect me, Never*
>   *neglect me.*
> *I am God's child.* (Henry, 1991)

It was hard to leave a Saturday meeting at Operation Breadbasket not feeling uplifted and energized.

In the mid-1960s, King had encouraged talented Black leaders to take on political leadership. He said, "They and many others must move out into political life as candidates and infuse it with their humanity, their honesty and their vision" (Ibid.). Jackson was at the forefront of those Black leaders who moved from the pulpit to the podium. The young preacher not only used his connection with King as a base for his secular leadership, but he also shared several of King's goals.

King and Jackson aligned on at least four basic beliefs: the supremacy of moral vision, the primacy of racism as a problem, the interdependence of all people, and individual self-respect. King's best-known speech, his "I Have a Dream" address at the 1963 March on Washington (MOW), is essentially a call for the nation to live up to its ideals. It evokes a dream or vision of a better future. Similarly, Jackson's nationally televised speech at the 1984 Democratic National Convention evokes this hope. He says, "What this campaign has shown above all else is that the key to our liberation is in our own hands and in our dream and vision of a better world." That vision, states Jackson, allows us to redeem each other and sustains us through dark times. "It is our hope that gives us a why for living when we do not see how to live" (Ibid.). By seeing the problem of racism as a fundamentally moral rather than a political or economic problem, they can assert the common humanity of all regardless of race or class. If people can recognize their common humanity, they can see the interdependence of all and overcome individual self-interest. However, to demand mutual respect and recognize a commonality of interest with others, one must have a clear sense of self-worth as a first step. One must say, "I am somebody, I am God's child."

If one views the problem of racism and inequality as essentially a moral issue, then being a minister of the gospel confers automatic legitimacy and authority. Jackson acknowledges the historic role of the church in the Black community. "The Black church," he says, "sustains black collectively by giving us a reason to live amid adversity and oppression" (Ibid.). In the political realm, however, bargaining or transactional politics is common practice. It can be difficult for a moral leader to compromise on an ideal and retain legitimacy.

Jackson had an advantage over Shirley Chisholm's 1972 presidential bid in his status as a Black male preacher. The Black church rallied around him in 1984 in a way it did not mobilize around Chisholm. His campaign rallies, at least one of which I attended in Oakland, were very much like his Breadbasket/PUSH meetings. There was preaching, gospel music, and, of course, taking up a collection for the campaign. While Jackson raised fewer funds than his main rivals, he was a master at drawing media attention rather than paying for political ads. By winning 85 percent of the Black vote nationwide, with little backing from Democratic Party regulars including Black mayors and the CBC, Jackson became a force to be dealt with inside the Democratic Party.

I was at the 1984 Democratic National Convention when Jackson challenged Mondale for the presidential nomination. I had managed to gain observer status as a researcher for my friend and former graduate school judo partner Jo Freeman's convention delegate project. While the outcome of the convention was preordained, the lobbying was still intense. Several Black elected officials asked the Jackson delegates to make a smart political decision and back Mondale. Most Jackson delegates felt they were on a moral crusade and would not compromise for political expediency. It was a position like that of the Mississippi Freedom Democratic Party (MFDP) in 1964 when they challenged the segregated Mississippi delegation and refused Lyndon Johnson's compromise of two token seats. I was surprised when at a caucus meeting of all the Black delegates, Andy Young and Coretta Scott King made a plea for all delegates to support Mondale. I was shocked when they were nearly booed off the stage. Only the arrival and intervention of Jackson enabled them to save face.

In prime time on July 18, 1984, Jackson delivered a long and eloquent address. After recounting the peaks and valleys of his campaign, he recalled a visit to my old boss, Hubert Humphrey. Jackson said, "I went to see Hubert Humphrey three days before he died. He had just called Richard Nixon from his dying bed, and many people wondered why. I asked him. He said, 'Jesse, from this vantage point, with the sun setting in my life, all of the speeches, the political conventions, the crowds and the great fights are behind me now. At a time like this you are forced to deal with your irreducible essence, forced to grapple with that which is really important to you. And what I have concluded about life,' Hubert Humphrey said, 'when all is said and done, we must forgive each other, and redeem each other, and move on.'" Jackson continued, "that America is not like a blanket—one piece of unbroken cloth, the same color, the same texture, the same size. America is more like a quilt—many patches, many pieces, many colors, many sizes, all woven together by a common thread." He called this a Rainbow Coalition and said Dr. King and Rabbi Abraham Heschel were crying out from their graves for us to reach common ground. There was not a dry eye in the convention hall as in conclusion Jackson raised his voice and shouted, "Suffering breeds character. Character breeds faith, and in the end faith will not disappoint. Our time has come. Our faith, hope and dreams have prevailed. Our time has come. Weeping has endured for nights but that joy cometh in the morning…" (www.pbs.org/wgbh/pages/frontline/jesse/speeches/jesse/speeches/jesse84speech.html)

While Jackson recalls King's appeal to the American Dream and the role of redemptive suffering, his goal of common ground is more political and less idealistic than King's Beloved Community. King's theology of "personalism" held that each individual was created in the image of God and therefore inseparably bound together. Segregation was sinful because it destroyed the wholeness of God. Love, or agape (disinterested love), was the glue that bound the individuals of the Beloved Community together. Jackson's vision of the ideal society, on the other hand, rests on shared interests in a state of pluralistic individuality rather than an integrated whole. Jackson takes a Niebuhrian view of the state as capable of justice, but not love. His speech at the 1988 Democratic National Convention in Atlanta (which I attended), entitled "A Call to Common Ground", reflects even more the pragmatism of a politician rather than the idealism of a preacher and lacks the emotional impact of the 1984 speech.

It was another Chicago politician who took the call for common ground to another level. Twenty years after Jackson's historic 1984 convention speech, Barack Obama would electrify delegates at the 2004 Democratic National Convention in Boston with his keynote address. He would contend that there are "no blue states or red states, only the United States". Obama immediately became a contender for the presidential nomination in 2008 and followed the speech with a book entitled *The Audacity of Hope*. The book's title was taken from a sermon by Reverend Jeremiah Wright, the Obama family minister who would play a controversial role in Obama's presidential campaign. In the book, Obama calls for an end to bitter partisanship and adopts the role of a pragmatic problem solver. Obama's election in 2008 rests in part on Jackson's success in increasing Black electoral participation and making the nominating process more open to insurgent candidates. I was in attendance as a reporter for *The Black Scholar* journal on August 23, 2008, when Obama accepted his party's nomination for president. In addition to the weeping in San Francisco in 1984, there was a sense of pride in the campaign Jackson had run. However, there was no jubilation because he lost the nomination. In fact, many Jackson delegates believed Mondale had conceded little to Jackson's demands.

The atmosphere in Denver was different. Many political observers, including me, did not believe Obama could win the nomination, let alone the election. In this regard, knowing too much Black political history may have been a liability. Rather than challenging Obama delegates, both Bill and Hillary Clinton gave speeches endorsing his candidacy and asked Hillary's delegates to make the nomination unanimous. In Denver I witnessed jubilation.

Walking into the stadium with a long line of Obama supporters, I met a Black woman in her eighties, dressed head-to-toe in hot pink, who said she had to be here. She rejected offers to carry her bags and said she had driven non-stop from Southern California by herself to witness Obama's nomination.

I'm not sure whether it was planned or not, but the nomination came exactly 45 years to the day of the March on Washington. When John Lewis strode onto the stage to introduce Obama, it seemed that a circle had been closed and a new door opened. Lewis was the only one of the "Big Five" civil rights leaders from the MOW still alive. As SNCC's leader, he had been the youngest and most outspoken of the leaders and had been pressured to tone down his criticism of the Kennedy administration. Now,

Obama, who was two years old in 1963, would *be* the administration. Lewis had wanted to end his MOW speech with the line "We shall crack the South into a thousand pieces and put them back together in the image of democracy (Henry, 2011, p. 4)." He had agreed to drop that line, but the anger of young activists toward an administration that refused to protect them remained.

Lewis had been a part of the transition from movement politics to electoral politics. Instead of smashing Atlanta, he represented it in Congress. In fact, Lewis was known by both Democrats and Republicans as the conscience of Congress. I met Lewis briefly in the early 1990s when I (along with the State Department's John Arbogast and Malcolm X's daughter Malaak was lobbying Congress to create a National African American History Museum. For several years, Lewis had introduced such legislation but found little support in the Senate or Clinton White House. Lewis eventually found a Republican Senate co-sponsor, Sam Brownback, and the bill was passed and signed by President George W. Bush. Lewis was now the "old lion" criticized by younger Black politicians for his early support of Hillary Clinton. Like the Black politicians who were reluctant to support Jesse Jackson, Lewis wanted to go with a winner. He switched his support to Obama in the middle of the primary elections, ending up, as he might say, on the right side of history.

As Lewis addressed the 84,000 Obama supporters in the Denver twilight, he said, "We are making a major down payment on the fulfillment of that (King's) dream. He continued that we were witnessing "the continuation of a struggle that began centuries ago in Lexington and Concord, in Gettysburg and Topeka, Kansas, in Philadelphia, Mississippi, and Selma, Alabama". Concluding, Lewis claimed, "Democracy is not a state. It is an act. It is a series of actions we must take to build what Martin Luther King, Jr., called the Beloved Community—a society based on simple justice that values the dignity and worth of every human being" (Ibid). After that, Obama's address was anti-climactic.

8
Beyond the ivory tower

I was sleeping late because it was August 17th, my 45th birthday. I heard the phone ring and my wife pick it up. She yelled, Charles, it's the McArthur Foundation calling. Hallelujah! I sprang to my feet and ran to the phone. Finally, I thought, my brilliant work in political science and Black Studies had been recognized. I grabbed the phone and said, this is Charles Henry. They said, would you be interested in being the director of the MacArthur Fellows program. Hiding my disappointment, I said yes.

It turned out that Dianne Pinderhughes, my old classmate from graduate school, who was then teaching at the University of Illinois, had recommended me. I thought it would be interesting to distribute funds for a change rather than apply for them. Think of all the new friends I would suddenly attract! I could take a leave of absence from Berkeley for a couple of years, and if I didn't like the job, I could come back. Thus began a long courtship.

Beginning that fall, I traveled to the Chicago headquarters of the MacArthur Foundation three times for interviews. I was also interviewed twice on the Berkeley campus. In those interviews, I learned the complex process of how the fellows program worked. Of course, the fellowship is popularly known as the "genius" award, then granting roughly $500,000 to recipients over five years with no restrictions on how the funds are spent. The foundation hopes you will use it to further your work, but purchasing a new luxury car might make you feel better about your work—no problem. You can't apply for the award; you must be nominated. The nominations are made by a fairly large and secret group of experts in various fields. A smaller group then narrows the pool to a group of finalists. The head of the nominating committee came to Berkeley to fill me in on the process. Later, a Berkeley faculty member involved in the selection process met with me.

After the first, fairly routine, interview at McArthur headquarters, I was invited back for a second interview. At that interview, I was handed an employee packet with information about health care and retirement plans. I also met with a senior vice president who asked me an unsettling question: could I view all nominations fairly without regard to race? I said I could while I thought that White candidates were probably not asked that question. It reminded me of the massive Carnegie study on race relations in the early 1940s, which selected Swedish economist Gunnar Myrdal to conduct it because they believed an African American would be biased. Apparently, we had not progressed far in the foundation world. A final meeting with the foundation president at her home was arranged for early April 1993. I was led to believe that it was more of a get-to-know-you meeting rather than an interview. The meeting was cordial, I thought, but a few weeks later I got a call saying the foundation was rethinking the position and thanks for your time.

The executive placement firm that McArthur hired to recruit for the position felt so badly about McArthur's decision (or non-decision) that they nominated me for a seat on the National Council for the Humanities. The firm was involved in nominating council candidates for the National Endowment for the Humanities (NEH) and National Endowment for the Arts (NEA), and not wanting a repeat of the McArthur experience, they had apparently vetted my nomination all the way to the White House. The council position requires a presidential appointment with Senate confirmation and clearance by the FBI. My interview for the council seat would turn out to be more thorough than the one I had later at the State Department. The FBI interviewed my old Sunday school teacher, Julius Richardson, as well as one of my former students, Ronnie Stevenson. When they asked Ronnie whether I had ever done anything that might embarrass President Clinton, Ronnie said no, but the president has done things that embarrass Professor Henry! I still got the nomination!!

The National Endowment for the Humanities, which the council oversees, is, by far, the largest funder of humanities projects in the United States. Membership on the council is staggered in six-year terms. When I started my term in 1994, there were still hold-overs from the Bush administration when Lynne Cheney had been chair. Under Cheney and her predecessor, William Bennett, NEH had been a key part of the "culture wars". This made for some contentious meetings as the Bush appointees opposed funding projects dealing with gender studies and ethnic studies. First under the leadership of Shelton Hackney and later under William Ferris, NEH funded some of the new directions in the humanities as well as the "classics" of Western culture. Since the National

Photo 13 Charles and others being sworn in at NEH (1996)

Humanities Council was advisory to the chair, he or she was free to ignore our recommendations.

Most of the council's work was done through committees overseeing the divisions of the federal agency. My first committee assignment was public projects. Public projects included funding many of the documentaries seen on public television, including Ken Burns's 1990 film "The Civil War". In the 20-plus-year history of NEH, Burn's film was the only one successful enough to return funds to NEH. This meant that Burns was likely to have any project he proposed to NEH funded. His documentary series on "Baseball", for example, was enthusiastically embraced by NEH. They hosted a reception on Capitol Hill for the film, accompanied by former Negro League star Buck Leonard. I later joined the committee with oversight of NEH's library funding. It soon became clear to me that funding library projects was a key to the agency's continued existence. Every congressional district contained libraries. Whenever NEH funding was threatened, as it often was along with our sister agency, the National Endowment for the Arts (NEA), members of Congress heard from their local libraries, and we were generally saved from budget slashing.

In addition to the routine funding of the many proposals NEH received, there were two prestigious awards bestowed every year. The National Humanities Medal was given to up to twelve recipients by the president on the recommendation of the council. It was always special to go to the White House for the award ceremony and meet the awardees. Often the recipients included popular novelists and performers as well as scholars. I especially remember a council discussion about potential awardees at which the chair asked who the number one Black scholar/intellectual of the day was. I objected to the notion that we could rank scholars and asked for what other racial/ethnic groups did we use such ranking. My preference was to reward older scholars who had paved the way for some of today's "star" public intellectuals. I was pleased that during my tenure on the council, librarian Dorothy Porter Wesley of Howard University and historian Benjamin Quarles of Morgan State University received the National Humanities Medal.

The other major award bestowed by NEH was the Jefferson Lecture on the Humanities. The distinguished scholar selected for the award received an honorarium and delivered a public lecture, usually at the Kennedy Center, although I remember my old professor John Hope Franklin delivering the lecture at the Daughters of the American Revolution (DAR) hall when he won in 1976. I also remember talks by novelist Toni Morrison and poet Gwendolyn Brooks during my six years on the council. My service on the council was, in some sense, an acknowledgment of the agency that had funded part of my graduate and post-graduate education.

Another academic who was in Washington during that time was the former chancellor of UC Berkeley, Michael Heyman. He was now the Secretary of the Smithsonian, and I bumped into him at an NEH event. Heyman invited me to lunch at the Smithsonian. I got a tour of his office as well as a history lesson on the founding of the Smithsonian. Heyman was anxious to get back to California and retire at his place on Stinson Beach. However, I did get him to agree to a meeting a few months later on the need for a national African American history museum. Joined by my State Department colleague and friend, John Arbogast, and Malcolm X's daughter, Malaak, we urged Heyman to pressure Congress for action. Since the Congressional Black Caucus had recently turned down the repurposing of an old Smithsonian building and Heyman was on his way out, he was not encouraging about the prospects.

The same year I joined the National Humanities Council, I moved to Washington to join the State Department in the summer of 1994. My friend John Shattuck had been appointed Assistant Secretary of State for Democracy, Human Rights and Labor (DRL) and urged me to come to Washington to fight for human rights on the inside rather than the outside of government. After eight years of Reagan and four years of George H. W. Bush, I couldn't resist. I had already been a part of the US delegation to the UN

World Conference on Human Rights. Loretta and the children stayed in Oakland, so I rented a small apartment on Capitol Hill.

DRL was the newest and smallest bureau of the units that make up the State Department bureaucracy. John created a position for me as director of the Office of External Affairs and Analysis in DRL. Like John, I was a political appointee, and my staff included three civil service professionals and a secretary as well as an intern. One staff member worked on democracy projects, another wrote speeches and press statements for John, and the third served as a congressional liaison. There was some delay in approving the position because my salary at Berkeley was significantly below the government pay grade scale for my position. I eventually got my office with a view, a television (status symbol), a safe, and a stack of classified covers. The most secret document I saw was a list of which government officials should attend the funeral of any number of elderly foreign leaders. Of course, if the list were public, the United States would have been implicated in their death. Although my position would be considered mid-level, my rank was among the highest for African Americans at State—the least integrated of all federal agencies. Although Clifford Wharton, Jr., had been deputy secretary of state from January 1993 to November 1993 and Vernon Jordan, Jr., had been a member of Clinton's transition team, they had little impact on diversifying the Foreign Service or the number of Black political appointees.

The daily routine was fairly flexible with one exception. Every morning there was a press sheet on my desk that listed the main stories in publications that mattered, for example, *The New York*

Times, *The Wall Street Journal*, *The Washington Post*, *The New Republic*, and so on. If the story involved human rights, I had to make sure we were prepared to respond to media inquiries. One morning there was a copy of an article on my desk with a memo from Undersecretary Wirth that everyone at my level needed to read. The article was entitled "The Coming Anarchy" by Robert Kaplan, and it appeared in *The Atlantic Monthly* (later it was expanded into a book). Kaplan was soon invited to give a talk at State about his work, and we were expected to attend. I made a mental note of the power of journalists to influence foreign policy. Had I drafted a similar memo and sent it up the hierarchy, I doubt it would have made it to Wirth.

The scope of our expected expertise seemed extremely broad; however, I soon realized how shallow it could be. This hit home to me one day when I informed John that someone from our bureau was expected to testify on a bill involving the national disabilities act. I asked John who our expert on the rights of the disabled was, and he said, "You are." I had two days to prepare a statement to be read by me at the Congressional hearing laying out DRL's position. Testifying with me would be people who had some real experience with disabilities, including Justin Dart, Jr., who some called the "father of the American Disabilities Act". I read my statement and then held my breath as I waited for questions. I breathed a sigh of relief when there were none. After the hearing, Dart approached me and said he was happy that someone with a human rights background was working at the State Department. Later I became DRL's instant expert on indigenous rights and held several meetings with indigenous groups.

My ties to human rights NGOs and AI specifically proved helpful that fall as the Clinton administration tried to decide whether to intervene in the political upheaval in Haiti. John was invited to the White House to advise Clinton on the problem and wanted some pictures showing the personal consequences of violence in Haiti. The government only had satellite images, and John asked me to find more graphic photos. I called AI, and they were able to provide me with some photos, which I passed on to John for his meeting. I also talked to Mike Levy from AI's co-group on Haiti, who was among Aristide's advisors for their perspective on an intervention. I provided John with the photos and perspective, and he said Clinton was moved by the images. The human rights community itself was split on whether the US should intervene or not.

A human rights education project I tried failed to achieve liftoff. Somehow, I became aware of the street law program designed to educate high school students on civil and legal rights through interactive learning. Started by law students at Georgetown University in 1972, Street Law produced a popular textbook in 1975 and by the mid-1980s had spread to 46 other countries. I obtained a copy of the textbook and met with Ed O'Brien, a former Georgetown Law student and co-founder of Street Law Inc., to discuss how the State Department could make human rights treaties more accessible to a general audience in the same way that Street Law showed high school students how our legal system impacted their daily lives. In short, given that the Justice Department knew little about CERD (see Chapter 10), I was certain it would fail to be ratified unless we did some human rights education for the general public. O'Brien was encouraging, but after checking with the state's legal bureau and several other lawyers, the project proved impossible to pull off in my short time at DRL.

My experience in writing a presidential statement to mark International Human Rights Day, December 10th, proved instructive. The statement is an annual affair in which the president makes some general statements of support for human rights. Once, as chair of AIUSA during the Reagan administration, I was invited to the White House for a small meeting of human rights NGOs on International Human Rights Day. President Reagan was to make a statement, and each of the NGOs was to be given two minutes to make a statement. I declined to make a cross-country trip to read a two-minute statement, and AIUSA sent our DC office director in my place. Later, when I asked how the meeting went, she replied that Reagan dozed off before all the statements were read, but Colin Powell took notes.

Clinton did not convene a meeting the year I prepared his statement, which was to be entered into the Federal Register and sent to our embassies. I reviewed some of his previous statements on human rights and cobbled together a general statement based on them. My draft had to go through six layers of bureaucracy at the State before it was sent to the White House. After it was returned several days later, I barely recognized it. Large sections had been eliminated or changed. When I asked why, the answer was the president had changed some of his views. I thought it might have been nice if he had informed the State Department.

I had more luck with an "Introduction to Human Rights" that the United States Information Agency (USIA) produced to be distributed to our embassies worldwide. The embassies in turn could make the publication available to visitors or anyone asking for information on human rights. Working with Rick Marshall and David Pitts at USIA, we produced a fifty-page booklet containing statements by President Clinton and Assistant Secretary Shattuck along with information about the Helsinki Process, Human Rights Watch, War Crimes Tribunal, Declaration of Independence, Bill of Rights, and the Four Freedoms. Philosopher Jack Donnelly contributed a piece on the meaning of human rights, and I was especially proud of the diversity of the twelve great human rights advocates we profiled.

Another outreach effort involved a speech in Croatia. My former AIUSA board colleague, Professor Winston Nagan, invited me to deliver a talk on nonviolence—focusing on the American civil rights movement—at the Inter-European University in Dubrovnik, Croatia, in late April. It was in the middle of the Bosnian conflict, but a truce had been declared, and it was deemed safe to travel. I flew from DC to Split via Zagreb, Croatia, and met another professor who was also going to Dubrovnik. A van was waiting to take us on a scenic drive down the coast. We passed several places that looked like resorts and were told that the Communist Party leaders and workers who had been awarded vacation prizes had been the main clients of these properties on the Adriatic Sea before the fall of the Soviet Union. I met Winston late that evening in a hotel across the bay from the old city.

At dawn, I was awakened by air raid sirens. Both Winston and I ran out of our rooms and went to the desk. We were told the truce had ended, and there was a warning that shelling might begin.

Although we knew the truce was coming to an end, no one thought hostilities would resume so soon. The Bosnian War from 1992 to 1995 had been sparked by the breakup of Yugoslavia. Early in the war, the Yugoslav People's Army (JNA) had shelled Croatian forces defending the key city of Dubrovnik in southern Croatia. The Old Town in Dubrovnik is a UNESCO World Heritage Site, and its shelling had provoked international outrage.

We were told a van would be headed back to Split very soon, and Winston and I quickly said we would be on it. We rushed to pack, and as the van pulled out of the area, we saw UN military personnel coming in. The drive back to Split seemed less scenic. When we got to the airport, we were told that international flights had been canceled. The only options were an overnight open-deck ferry ride to Italy or going out on a flight with UN troops. Winston told me to flash my diplomatic passport. I did with no luck—we were told the UN flights were full. Finally, we found one civilian flight leaving for Slovenia and took it. Arriving in Ljubljana late that night, we found a hotel and returned to the airport early the next morning. After making a connection in Amsterdam, I arrived in Washington, which was buried in the heaviest snowfall in years. The moral of the story is that it is difficult to talk about nonviolence in the middle of a war.

I think I learned a lot about how government works and doesn't work in my short time at State. The bureaucracy moved slowly through many layers. Foreign policy direction seemed to come from the White House and its National Security Council, with State often playing catch-up. My Human Rights Day statement was a trivial example of the process. Moreover, we were relatively underfunded. A very small percentage of funding went to non-military foreign aid. Even our embassies appeared underfunded. I once attended a meeting called by Undersecretary Wirth that raised the possibility of having some of our consulates funded by corporations, for example, an adopt-a-country program!

Perhaps the best example of underfunding was the state's computer network. We tended to get old model hardware that had been passed down from the Pentagon. I had the distinction of being in the last class trained in the WANG computer programming language. It had finally dawned on someone with authority that using the WANG system made it difficult to communicate with other federal agencies, let alone the rest of the world. Just as I was leaving, State got permission to switch to Apple or Microsoft. However, it was left to each bureau to choose a system, which meant that the bureaus would still have a problem if one had Apple and the other Microsoft. Why wouldn't the Secretary of State or some other authority simply say one or the other? This failure to choose seemed to reflect a larger problem. There were a lot of smart people doing a lot of unnecessary work because no one wanted to take responsibility.

One of the smart people I ran into at State was Tom Malinowski. Tom had been a student in my course on Martin Luther King at Berkeley. As part of the course, students had to do a project involving public service. Tom had launched what became a nationwide campaign to register students to vote. Later that project was part of his application for a Rhodes scholarship. Tom was awarded the scholarship, and after two years at Oxford, he had worked for Senator Daniel Moynihan. Tom was now a speechwriter for

Christopher. He would go on to be Assistant Secretary of State for Human Rights (DRL) and then be elected to Congress from New Jersey. Another former student of mine, Tuhin Roy, was working for Human Rights Watch while I was a state.

The frustration of trying to promote human rights from inside the government came to a head when the Republicans, led by Newt Gingrich, took control of Congress in November 1994. I got a sense of what might happen when John wrote a preface (largely drafted by me) to the US report on the International Covenant on Political and Civil Rights. When the report, along with the preface, was finally printed in September, conservatives were shocked when we admitted the US did not have a perfect record on human rights. Former Reagan administration official Midge Decter accused him of "moral greed", a term I had never heard before. When former vice-presidential candidate Geraldine Ferraro came up for confirmation of her appointment as US ambassador to the UN Human Rights Commission in Geneva, Helms asked her forty questions meant to stall the nomination. Those questions came to me to answer before the conclusion of the hearing the next day. Half of them were on the ICCPR report and the rest on questions like how many countries in the world have an official language—Helms was promoting English as the official language of the US. As I sat at my desk late that night, I began to question my decision to work at State. The Republican Congressional victories in the November election meant that Senator Jesse Helms took over as chair of the Senate Foreign Affairs Committee, ending any prospect of advancing human rights treaties.

There were some real perks to the job. In September 1994, I was on the White House lawn to welcome Russian President Boris Yeltsin to the White House. Political appointees were encouraged to be part of this secure and friendly audience for formal state visits. Yeltsin later came to the State Department for meetings. A month later, the process repeated itself for the state visit of Nelson Mandela. I distinctly remember Mandela appearing on the balcony with Clinton and saying, only half-jokingly, that he had come to pick up a blank check for South Africa.

My last major project for DRL was a conference on human rights for NGOs to be hosted by the State Department. I coordinated the conference, which was to be held on April 3rd. Secretary of State Warren Christopher, UN Ambassador Madeline Albright, and Undersecretary Tim Wirth were all featured along with John. Well over 200 participants were confirmed. Unfortunately, I caught the flu a couple of days before the conference and had not recovered by conference day. Nonetheless, I dragged myself to work, and despite Christopher's late arrival, I tried to keep things on track until I left for home during the last afternoon sessions. Everyone declared the conference a success; however, by then I had already told John I would be returning to Berkeley by the end of June. He understood and threw a memorable going-away party for me, including staff, who signed a giant State Department seal for me, and some NGO friends.

Photo 14 Charles and John Shattuck at the State Department (1995)

9
Education abroad

The type of power the State Department exercises abroad is often called "soft" power as compared to the "hard" power of the Defense Department. One of the most effective government programs administered through the State Department has been the Fulbright fellowships, named for the Arkansas senator who helped create them in 1946. Since its inception, over 400,000 students and faculty have studied in 190 countries. I have been fortunate to receive two Fulbright Distinguished Chair Fellowships—one to Bologna, Italy, in 2003 and another to Tours, France, in 2006. The Fulbright Distinguished Chair Fellowship is distinct from the Fulbright Research Fellowship in that it lets you teach a course in English for a semester.

Loretta and I moved to Bologna in January 2003 for the spring semester at the University of Bologna. Our host, Tiziano Bonazzi, a professor of American history, had secured an apartment for us in the old city near the university. From our window we could see a thousand-year-old Christian church built on top of an early Roman church—we went there for Easter service. The old city is largely covered by porticos. In the early days of the university, students were often housed in rooms constructed over the sidewalks to save space. The university itself is spread out in old palazzos housing various departments and professional schools throughout the old city. Founded in 1088, Bologna is the oldest university in the Western world. Among its graduates and faculty were Copernicus, Galvani, Pope Gregory XIII, Petrarch, Volta, Cassini, and more recently, Umberto Eco. When I asked if I was the first person of African descent to teach at the university, I was quickly informed that a famous Muslim scholar from Africa was at the university in the Middle Ages.

I taught a weekly course entitled "Human Rights, Martin Luther King, and U.S. Foreign Policy" to students who all spoke English. In fact, a couple were American exchange students. My office had frescoes on the ceiling, and there was an elevator just for faculty. My appointment was at the Department of Politics, Institutions, and History, which was housed in a beautiful old palazzo. I only regretted that it was impossible to get the students to ask questions or engage in discussion. They had been trained to listen carefully and take notes. The distance between the professor and the student was too great to engage in dialogue. It was a sharp contrast from Berkeley, where students challenged me from day one.

When the Fulbright scholars in Italy met for an orientation at the American Academy in Rome, I was introduced to the American ambassador to Italy. He was a real estate tycoon specializing in shopping centers who, like me, spoke no Italian. After some talk about tennis and the State Department, he said I must be comfortable in Bologna, the Berkeley of Italy. Eurostar trains made it easy for Loretta and me to travel to Rome, Venice, Milan, Florence, and Naples. The latter trip came about through meeting another Fulbright scholar at the Rome orientation. She had a cousin living in Naples and invited us to join her on a visit. The highlight for me, despite being inappropriately dressed, was attending an opera at Naples' historic opera house. We also squeezed in a boat trip to the isle of Capri off the coast of Naples.

Bologna's location made short trips to Egypt, Turkey, and Greece possible. Egypt's tourism industry was still recovering from a terrorist attack that killed a number of German tourists a few years earlier. We flew from Cairo to Aswan to take a cruise down the Nile. Many empty cruise boats were docked along the shore. It's hard to escape the feeling of antiquity floating down the Nile. Starting at Abu Simbel with the giant statues of Ramses II, you witness dows on the water and ox carts on the shore, much as you would have two thousand years ago. We stopped at the great temples of Karnak and the Valley of the Kings. When we reached Cairo, we were surprised at how close the city was to the Great Pyramids. They were across the street from our hotel. Yet when you stand in front of the Sphinx for the nighttime light show and the announcer says you are standing where Alexander the Great, Julius Caesar, Napoleon, and countless others have stood, the timelessness of the place hits home. I had seen so many Egyptian statues and artifacts in the great museums of Europe and America that I was afraid nothing would be left in Egypt. When we toured the National Museum in Cairo, however, you could barely move without bumping into some priceless object. And we were told that only about ten percent of Egypt's ancient treasures have been excavated.

Our trip to Turkey was almost as overwhelming as Egypt. Istanbul, situated on the Bosporus between Europe and Asia, has been a crossroad of many cultures since the days of the Silk Road.

Founded as Byzantium in the seventh century BCE and then renamed Constantinople by the Roman Emperor Constantine, Istanbul is now the most visited city in the world and the largest in Europe. Our quick visit to the immense Hagia Sophia, the beautiful Blue Mosque, and the Topkapi Palace made us feel like we were just scratching the surface of the country's culture. Going across the bridge connecting the European side of the city with the Asian side and cruising on a boat between the two was a magical feeling.

Our trip to Greece came at a bad time. Athens was preparing for the Olympics, and several of the best museums were closed for renovation. Moreover, a strike by transportation workers over the war in Iraq made it difficult to get around. Nonetheless, we were able to visit the Acropolis, Greek parliament, and the stadium where the modern Olympics was renewed in 1896. We ended our trip with a tour of three Greek islands, including a visit to the Blue Grotto.

Just before finishing my Fulbright stay in Italy, USIA invited me to give two lectures in Sicily. It was beautiful spring weather when Loretta and I landed in Palermo and were met by someone from the US consulate office. We had a couple of days to explore Palermo, its famous opera house (seen in Godfather II), and the mosaics at Monreale before being driven across the island to Ragusa and Catania. On the way to the universities in these two cities, we stopped at a famous Roman villa to admire mosaics. Some featured hunting scenes while others depicted sporting events seen in the Olympic Games. We spent a night in Ragusa, a beautiful old hill city with great limoncello, before heading to Catania at the foot of Mt. Etna. In fact, that very active volcano was spewing ash, and there was some concern that our flight back to Bologna might be delayed; however, we made it back safely.

Loretta and I enjoyed our experience in Italy so much I decided to apply for another Fulbright Distinguished Chair. In 2006, I was awarded one of the first Distinguished Fulbright–Tocqueville Chairs in France. My location was the University of Tours, formerly Francois Rabelais University, founded in 1969, almost 900 years after the University of Bologna. The buildings were modern concrete structures housing over 30,000 students. My host was Claudine Raynaud, an American literature professor, and I was attached to the English Department. The university found us an apartment across the Loire River from the central city. My walk to work involved crossing the Loire on a long footbridge.

I taught a course entitled "Racial Reparations" to English-speaking students. Once again, I generally failed to get them to ask questions or engage in dialogue. However, just the opposite happened when I gave a public talk on reparations. Near the end of the fall semester, my hosts convened a day-long mini-conference on the topic. I kicked off the discussion with a talk on my research—my book on the topic was published a year later. When I finished my remarks, a woman stood up and said something like, everything you have said is illegal. Puzzled, I asked her for an explanation. She said it was illegal in France to collect data identifiable by race. Moreover, raising the topic of racial reparations was divisive. Others disagreed with her, and after some discussion, the mini-conference proceeded, and I avoided any jail time. In fact, I was invited by the prestigious Sciences Po in Paris, France's leading social sciences university, to give virtually the same lecture. I also spoke at Paris Nanterre University, formerly Paris X, on the subject of reparations.

Fortunately, it was easy to get to Paris from Tours on the Eurostar bullet train. On one memorable trip early in the semester after a meeting with all the Fulbright scholars in France, a special reception was held by the French Senate honoring a law professor and me as the first two Fulbright–Tocqueville Distinguished Chairs. On another occasion, I was invited to the US ambassador's residence in Paris for a reception honoring Toni Morrison. Unfortunately, I lost my wallet in a taxi going to the reception but was pleasantly surprised when the taxi driver turned it in at a police station. Of course, Tours is the center of the Loire region, and we were able to visit several of the historic chateaus nearby. We were also able to visit Bordeaux, which was only two hours away by train. Our favorite trip within France was to Mont St. Michel. The Mont St. Michel Abbey dates from the Middle Ages and had welcomed pilgrims from all walks of life as well as several kings of England and France. During the French Revolution, it made a perfect prison since it is surrounded by water and accessible by land only at low tide. We stayed overnight in a historic inn and completed our trip with a visit to the beaches of Normandy. A somber time of reflection.

Even with all the traveling in France, we managed three brief foreign excursions. One was to Morocco for the international Fulbright conference in Marrakesh. We met more Fulbrighters from across the globe and walked between snake charmers in the main square to get to the narrow passageways of the Kasbah.

Another trip found us in Spain. We started in Barcelona, which we loved from a previous visit in 1972. It's impossible to overstate the grandeur of Antoni Gaudi's Cathedral de Sagrada Familia or the charm of a walk down the La Rambla. From Barcelona, we took a train to Madrid. The train trip allowed us to see the Spanish countryside. A personal highlight in Madrid was the opportunity to buy a classical guitar from the guitar maker's workshop. At the end of our semester in France, we squeezed in a trip to London with a friend at Christmas time.

The Fulbright Distinguished Chairs were a semester long. Enough time to feel like you were no longer a tourist, but certainly not enough time to immerse yourself in the culture—especially if you didn't speak the language. My department sponsored even shorter, five-week summer sessions in the African diaspora. I taught three of them—Barbados in 1996, Zimbabwe in 1998, and Cuba in 2002. In several ways, Cuba was the most interesting and challenging experience, although they all had something to offer.

The Cuba course was new and required a visit to Cuba the year before to make arrangements. Berkeley already offered a summer session Spanish language course in Cuba; however, our course was focused on the culture and taught in English. To help me plan for the course, I asked an old friend, Robert Chrisman, publisher of *The Black Scholar* journal, and Alan Caldwell, a graduate student who would serve as one of my teaching assistants, to join me. Both spoke Spanish, and Chrisman had been to Cuba several times and had excellent contacts, including the president of the National Assembly, Richard Alarcon. I timed our May visit with my participation in a UN conference on the Americas held at the Cuban Press Association. Prior to the start of the summer session, I held a meeting with enrolled students. I explained to them that there was no telephone service to the United States, that credit cards were not accepted, and there was no American embassy to call if they got in trouble.

Most of our administrative work was handled through the Casa de las Americas. At this time, the Clinton administration was allowing travel to Cuba for educational purposes. Along with Casa de Americas, the Fernando Ortiz Foundation assisted us in setting up a series of lectures on various aspects of Cuban life and culture. The title of the course was "Cuba and the African Diaspora." My lectures centered on the Black radical experience in Cuba. Toward that end, I had students read William Brent's *Long Time Gone*. Brent was a former Black Panther from Oakland who held the record for the longest airplane hijacking by a single individual—San Francisco to Havana in 1969.

After arriving in the summer of 2002, I met with the director of the Ortiz Institute to finalize our speakers. I mentioned to him that we were reading William Brent's work, and he said Bill lives not far from here. My teaching assistant, Lea Redmond, immediately said, I'm going to find him and bring him to class tomorrow. Sure enough, when I arrived at class, Bill Brent and Lea were waiting for me. I had never met someone on the FBI's ten most wanted list. Although Brent had dropped out of school in Oakland, he now held a doctorate in Spanish from the University of Havana. He had adjusted well to life in exile, but not all was positive for Blacks in Cuba. He was working on a book on the Black experience in

Photo 15 Charles with William Brent (2002)

Cuba. When I asked if he missed the US, he said not being able to attend his mother's funeral had been hard on him.

Brent's lecture was not my first inkling that racism was still an issue in Cuba despite being formally prohibited by the Constitution. When I visited in May 2001, Chrisman, Caldwell, and I were given a tour of the Martin Luther King Center in Havana. They worked in the poor Afro-Cuban community that the center was located in. The center was associated with an Ebenezer Baptist Church that had been visited by Rep. Charles Rangel, among others. Although Black general Antonio Maceo was widely acknowledged as one of the country's founders, it was easily seen that Black Cubans held most of the menial jobs and few of the white-collar positions. My White students were able to visit me in my hotel room, but when my Black teaching assistant tried to visit, he was held up at the front desk. I had to come down and vouch that he was American and not Cuban. Toward the end of the summer session, some students complained that all our guest lecturers had been White Cubans. When questioned about this, our hosts said we make no distinctions based on color; we are all Cubans. Ironically, I had been in Durban when Fidel Castro gave one of the best speeches I had ever heard on racial reparations at the UN World Conference on Race and Racial Discrimination in 2001. He launched a fierce critique of the consequences of colonialism. Yet any discussion of racial reparations in Cuba itself would have been forbidden.

The racial hierarchy was even more apparent when the class went on a field trip to the beach town of Varadero. As tourists crowded the hotels, they were waited on by Black staff with White managers. Another field trip to Santiago de Cuba was more complicated. The Afro-Cuban population is the majority in Santiago, and African culture was everywhere. We were fortunate to be there during the carnival. The main parade began around 9 pm and was still going strong when we left after midnight. The dancing, drumming, and costumes were all rooted in African culture. Just outside Santiago is San Juan Hill, where Teddy Roosevelt led a famous charge of his Rough Riders to secure a battle victory in the Spanish-American War. San Juan Hill had special meaning for me because my father had served with cavalrymen who had fought in that battle. They had secured the hill before Roosevelt made his famous charge. Later, during his presidency, Roosevelt would disparage the courage of Black troops.

Race relations in Zimbabwe were the opposite of the situation in Cuba when I taught a course entitled "Africa Unite: Pan

Africanism" in the summer of 1998 in Harare. Racial polariza-
tion seemed to have grown worse since my visit to Zimbabwe
for Amnesty International five years earlier, and Mugabe had
become more unpredictable. Of course, the major conflict was
between the landless Black majority and the small percentage of
White farmers who owned the most valuable agricultural land.
Berkeley, however, had conducted a summer session there in
1997 and believed it was safe to repeat in 1998.

The class met at a social science research institute on the out-
skirts of the capital, and our students stayed with Zimbabwean
families. Like Cuba, we arranged several guest lectures, including one by labor leader Morgan Tsvangirai, who would later be
elected president but be denied power by Mugabe. In addition
to the lectures, field trips to Chapungu Village (sculpture and
dance), Great Zimbabwe, Murewa Village, and Victoria Falls/
Hwange National Park were arranged.

It was at Victoria Falls that my male students and I had a narrow escape. After my students failed to convince me to bungee
jump off the high bridge over the Zambezi River gorge between
Zambia and Zimbabwe, I agreed to go white-water rafting with
them. What I didn't know at the time was that the Zambezi
below the falls is the roughest stretch of commercially rafted rapids in the world. Moreover, when the raft outfitters arrived to take
us down to the river, it was a cut-rate firm named Adrift. I had
told my teaching assistant to always bargain when shopping in
Africa, but I had not intended that advice to apply to river rafting.
Hiking down the steep banks to the river was risky itself. After
some minimal instructions, including how to use what looked

like war surplus life jackets, we set off with most of the men in one raft with a guide and the women in another raft with a guide. On our second rapid, called the three little pigs, the men's raft flipped over, tossing us into the air. I seemed to have trouble getting out of the rapid because the raft was on top of me. When I finally emerged, I was immediately swallowed by the second and then the third rapid. The safety kayak pulled up next to me, and I grabbed hold. As soon as I had a grip, one of the students grabbed onto me from behind, threatening to tip the kayak over. After I pried him off, I looked for the nearest land. What I saw was a big rock with a crocodile sitting on it. This gave me an immediate shot of adrenaline, and I swam in the opposite direction as fast as I could. The all-female kayak found all this greatly entertaining; however, once we had collected everyone, one of the women who had joined the men refused to go on. We had just started out, and the roughest rapids were still ahead of us with names like Oblivion and the Washing Machine. The guide said you can't walk out; you're in a national wildlife park with plenty of lions and other predators. He promised to get her through the rest of the trip, and she grabbed his leg and didn't let go until we left the river two hours later. The rest of our time in Zimbabwe was uneventful compared to rafting the Zambezi.

The summer session in Barbados in 1996 was very different from Cuba and Zimbabwe. Students were more interested in the beaches than the culture or politics. My course was entitled "Contemporary Black Leadership", but it was difficult to get the students to do any reading. It was not helpful that our sessions took place on the campus of the University of the West Indies at Cave Hill, which provided numerous distractions.

Photo 16 Charles and students on the Zambezi River (1998)

Barbados is generally regarded as one of the most British of the Anglophone Caribbean nations, and it seemed to reflect that reputation. We enjoyed high tea, for example, at the National Museum. There was one major exception. We were there during "crop over", which, much like a carnival in Cuba, drew heavily from African dancing and drumming. More recently, Barbados has moved away from England by cutting ties to the Commonwealth, promoting Pan-Africanism, and demanding reparations for slavery and colonialism. There seemed to be little interest in United States politics. I gave a public talk on the coming 1996 presidential election between Clinton and Dole that drew an audience of roughly half a dozen. Perhaps it was the speaker?

10
From palm wine to rock and roll

I was honored to be on the International Executive Committee (IEC), the governing board of Amnesty International (AI), from 1989 to 1991. One of my oversight responsibilities was our organization's work in Africa. Amnesty groups in Sierra Leone, a country established in 1787 to repatriate the formerly enslaved from England, were seeking full country section status. The groups were holding their annual meeting in Taima, a small village outside Freetown; the IEC was invited to send a representative, namely me, charged with evaluating whether they met certain criteria necessary for section status.

When I arrived, I found the airport was situated at the end of a long peninsula. Although Freetown was across the bay, there was no ferry. I took a long and very rough taxi ride to our office in the city, a room above a mechanic's garage with no electricity. There, in the candlelight, I met the head of the group and AI's staff person for West Africa. We took a taxi for the hour-plus ride to the meeting site.

The subsequent meeting was held in a large room at the village school. I was impressed that a population living largely on subsistence agriculture was willing to contribute their meager funds for stamps to send letters protesting human rights abuses of governments half a world away. They even had people fishing for AI.

At lunchtime, a special meal was arranged for the visitors, including two other international AI guests and me. The meal was my first taste of Sierra Leonean cuisine and included potato leaves—a dish our staff representative from Cameroon assured me was not something eaten in his country. Later in the afternoon, I was treated more like the common folk and invited to the school kitchen for some liquid refreshments. In the middle of the kitchen sat a huge kettle containing what I was told was freshly made palm wine, a national drink. People formed a circle around the kettle, and a common cup was produced for all of us to share. Before he dipped the cup into the kettle, our host reached into the palm wine and pulled out a large spider! He said the spider had been put in to eat any insects in the wine. He then proceeded to dip the cup into the wine and handed it to me to take the first drink.

This presented a diplomatic dilemma. I had been warned not to drink anything not bottled, including water. The palm wine was not only not bottled but had a spider swimming in it. Not wanting to offend our hosts, I bit the bullet and drank the wine— rather, I took a small sip. They asked me how I liked it, and I lied and said it was okay, but I had had better. They quite agreed, saying it needed to age more. I prepared to spend most of my remaining time in Sierra Leone in the latrine.

My accommodations were a room in the small cinder-block home of a local family. I was assigned a young girl as my personal servant and assured she would do anything to please me. I was also invited to contribute some funds to her school tuition, which I did, although not as much as originally suggested. Unfortunately, the toilet was outside in the rear of the house. I envisioned myself making numerous trips around the back of the house at night, dodging snakes and other wildlife. Fortunately, there were no ill effects from the palm wine; apparently, the spider did a good job!

A year later, a terrible civil war erupted in Sierra Leone that lasted 11 years and witnessed many gross violations of human rights. I still wonder what happened to the young girl.

When the IEC approved Sierra Leone's application for section status later that year, it became the 46th national section. At that time, Amnesty International had over a million members in 150 countries and more than 6,000 volunteer groups in 70 countries. Twenty-five sections of the 46 national sections were in Latin America, Asia, Africa, and the Middle East, but only 15 were self-sustaining. The five most developed sections provided the bulk of funding for Amnesty's headquarters, the International Secretariat (IS) in London. The 270 staff at the IS were primarily concerned with researching prisoner cases. The information the IS provided was sent to volunteer groups to be used in letter-writing on behalf of prisoners of conscience (POC) and urgent actions on behalf of those tortured or disappeared. Only two per-cent of the budget was devoted to development work.

The problems facing the groups in Sierra Leone were the same problems AI faced in developing a global human rights move-ment. While AI was scrupulous in maintaining ideological neutral-ity, its methods confined it to a rather narrow base of educated,

Photo 17 Charles at an AI meeting in Sierra Leone (1989)

middle-class volunteers. The technique of letter-writing, for example, excluded much of the non-literate population of the world, including Sierra Leone, where only 20 percent of the population was literate. Urgent Actions assumed that members had access to electronic mail, telegraph, or telephone communications, or at least reliable mail service. This was not the case in Sierra Leone or in much of the developing world. And when AI groups did form in less developed countries the members were often expatriates from Europe rather than the native population. Even in the United States, the Hawaiian groups were dominated by "haoles", residents from the mainland. If AI hoped to do a campaign around an issue like torture, it needed to provide audio-visual equipment for human rights education.

Members from Sierra Leone expressed frustration with IS staff, whom they felt controlled the African regional meeting in 1989. They believed their voices were not heard, and they were pushed into development plans that were unrealistic. An effort, for example, to sell AI calendars produced by the British section when there was no market for them in Sierra Leone. Instead, members would have preferred to produce their own products to be sold by British members in the United Kingdom. Not only did the IS need to listen to developing sections, but they might also need to be willing to work with government-sponsored elites to form national human rights organizations. Something the developed sections would never consider with their own governments.

Groups in developing sections might also consider working with mass indigenous movements or political elites who have human rights as only a part of their agenda. I had been sent to Zimbabwe by the IEC to attend a World Labor Congress meeting. The Mugabe government had ironically jailed Zimbabwe's best-known labor leader just before the Congress opened. I pleaded unsuccessfully with the minister of justice to have him released, and the World Congress passed a resolution condemning his imprisonment. Unfortunately, we had no AI section in Zimbabwe to apply pressure on the government.

I was more successful in my IEC emergency mission to Grenada. Are you a TV evangelist? That was the question the waiter asked my colleague and me as we ordered breakfast at the beachfront bar/café in Georgetown, Grenada. It was a good question since we had had our breakfast for the last two days dressed in suits and ties and never gone near the beach. You could say we were on a mission from God (cue the Blues Brothers), but we were only evangelists for human rights.

The Caribbean island of Grenada achieved its independence from the United Kingdom in 1974. Sir Eric Gairy had led the independence movement, and he and his party, the Grenada United Labor Party, claimed victory in a general election in 1976. However, the opposition group, called the New Jewel Movement (NJW), led by Maurice Bishop, did not accept the result as legitimate. An armed revolution ensued, and the NJM overthrew Gairy's government while he was out of the country on March 13, 1979.

The Bishop government began constructing the Point Salines International (later the Maurice Bishop) Airport with the help of Britain, Cuba, Libya, Algeria, and others. The American government accused Grenada of constructing facilities, including an especially long runway, to aid a Soviet–Cuban military buildup on the island. In 1983, Rep. Ron Dellums traveled to Grenada on a fact-finding mission at Bishop's invitation. He reported that the airport project was solely for economic development and not military use. Nonetheless, the Reagan administration continued to warn about the threat posed to the US and the Caribbean by the project.

On October 16, 1983, Deputy Prime Minister Bernard Coard and others seized power and placed Bishop under house arrest. There were mass protests against the coup, leading to Bishop's escape and attempt to reassert his authority. He was eventually recaptured and executed along with other supporters by a firing squad of soldiers. The army, under Hudson Austin, formed a military council to rule the country and placed Governor General Paul Scoon, the Queen's representative, under house arrest.

Scoon secretly asked for military assistance, and on October 25, the US led a coalition of Caribbean nations in an invasion code-named *Operation Urgent Fury*. The UN General Assembly, along with Canada, Trinidad and Tobago, and the UK, condemned it as "a flagrant violation of international law". After the inevitable US victory, thus vanquishing the Vietnam Syndrome, Scoon assumed interim power until new elections were held in December 1984.

Just after the Marines landed in Grenada, they arrested Coard and other members of his government. They were tried in August 1986 on charges of ordering the murder of Bishop and seven others. Coard, his wife, and 12 other co-conspirators were sentenced to death. A long appeal process began that ultimately reached the High Court in London in 1991. The court denied the appeal, and it was feared the prisoners would soon be executed.

It was at this point that I got a call from the London headquarters of Amnesty International. As a member of the International Executive Committee, they wanted me to go to Grenada to make a personal plea to the government to spare the lives of the condemned. Joining me on the mission would be London barrister

Lawrence Kershen, who had attended the appeal as an observer for AI.

Arriving in Georgetown, I was shocked to find that AI had reserved cabanas for us on the Grand Strand, the island's best beach. Normal AI accommodations were bare-bones hotels like the London Ryan or dorms. Later I would discover the only reason we were there was due to the hotel's dependable fax service.

Our first meeting was with members of AI's small group on the island. We had considered making an appeal to the Catholic Bishop to intervene given the public opposition to the death penalty by the Pope. We shelved that idea when the AI group told us the bishop of Grenada was firmly in favor of execution. Later we met with some family members of the prisoners. It became apparent that on a small island like Grenada, everyone was either related or knew each other.

At breakfast the next morning, we headed for our last meeting with Prime Minister Nicholas Brathwaite. He was very polite and listened to all our arguments. We told him that on an island where everyone was known, a new group of grieving families would only reignite the divisions of the past. He responded that he was torn over the issue, but there had to be some accountability. I countered that if there was any doubt, he should err on the side of life rather than irreversible death. My moral reasoning drew a hearty laugh!

We left Grenada discouraged. I think we both felt that at the very least the government would execute Coard as an example. A few days later I received another call from London. Brathwaite had commuted all the sentences! Of course, my partner and I claimed full credit, with maybe some intervention from heaven after all!

To some extent, the obstacles to developing AI in Sierra Leone, Zimbabwe, and Grenada mirrored my own experience in diversifying Amnesty in the United States. At the time I went to Sierra Leone, I had been an AI member for less than seven years. I think I first heard of the organization in 1977 when it won the Nobel Peace Prize. I was impressed that citizens had come together voluntarily to do something concrete to promote human rights. Given my political science background, I was a bit skeptical of the influence of letter-writing, but the point was moot since there were no AI groups in central Ohio. When I arrived at the University of California in the fall of 1981, Berkeley's Amnesty campus network was very visible, and I decided to attend a meeting toward the end of my first semester. A staff member, Sister Laola Hironaka, was the coordinator of AIUSA's oldest and largest campus network. There were no faculty in the group, and Laola was quickly drawn to me as a young African American professor interested in human rights.

By coincidence, AIUSA was holding its annual general meeting (AGM) in Seattle in the summer of 1982. A group of us from the Berkeley network decided to drive up for the meeting at Seattle University. It was an opportunity to hear AI's Secretary General and meet the members from other groups. One of the first people I met was AIUSA board member Bill Watanabe, director of the Little Tokyo Service Center in Los Angeles. Bill, who had been born in a Japanese internment camp and was AIUSA's first board member of color, encouraged me to run for the board. When

I replied that I thought long-time members might resent a new-comer running for the board, Bill said if they do, they won't vote for you. I couldn't deny the logic and agreed to run.

At my first board meeting in 1983, I met two other new board members who would become lifelong friends. Paul Hoffman, then the legal director for the American Civil Liberties Union (ACLU) in southern California, would often be my roommate at various meetings. We shared a passion for basketball and base-ball, which we worked into at least two meetings. John Shattuck was a vice president at Harvard when we met. John and I would try to play as much tennis as possible at each board meeting. These breaks for sports were essential to our mental health. It is hard to overstate the immense volume of paper to be consumed by each board member or the endless meetings we attended.

John (Jack) Healey was also attending his first board meeting as AIUSA's new executive director. Jack grew up in Pittsburgh, about a hundred miles from my hometown in Ohio. He had been a Catholic seminary student before becoming involved in human rights. Jack and the new board members, as well as most of the old board, seemed ready to push for an expanded, cultur-ally diverse AIUSA. In addition to Healey, I would work with staff members Curt Goering, Jack Rendler, Ali Miller, Charles Fulwood, and Nick Rizzi over the years in pushing change.

This new push for cultural diversification faced resistance from some long-time AI members. They were comfortable in their homes writing letters protesting the jailing of Soviet dissidents. They saw no need to try other techniques like national cam-paigns or targeting minority groups for recruitment.

In a 1986 memo to our new task force on cultural diversification, I pointed out that minorities were often not comfortable going to homes in predominantly White neighborhoods (I was once stopped by the police going to Ginetta Sagan's home) to write letters to far distant countries about human rights violations. I also mentioned that we already targeted groups like lawyers, doctors, and students with special recruitment efforts. Rather than regarding cultural diversification as affirmative action, I urged members to see it as both an opportunity to do human rights education and to make our existing work more effective both domestically and globally.

To be more effective, AI also needed to change with the times. Oppressive governments were becoming increasingly sophisticated in avoiding accountability. Instead of locking up prisoners of conscience, they "disappeared" them, with Argentina being a prime example. AI's Urgent Actions were developed to immediately spotlight those who disappeared or were tortured. In fact, with the move toward détente, the whole model of balancing prisoner cases between the East and West was becoming less relevant. Moreover, the number of non-state actors on the world stage was rapidly increasing. It was impossible to hold accountable or shame terrorist groups that had no permanent location and had not signed any human rights treaties.

To be effective in a changing world, the organization also needed to examine its own internal rules and procedures. For me, the rule that had the most impact on our growth was the prohibition against doing work in your own country (WOC). This rule probably made sense in AI's early years. Its main goal had been to insulate members in countries hostile to human rights from charges of subversion. They could rightly claim their activism was not directed at their own government. However, as AI grew in countries like the United States, it was a real obstacle in attracting minority group members. Since it also applied to staff, it meant that many of AI's most knowledgeable researchers could not work on the country they knew best—their own. After many task forces, commissions, and resolutions, the WOC rule was modified to allow working in our own countries.

During the last three years of my board service, our efforts at cultural diversification began to show results. A staff position was created to work with members on cultural diversification, and the staff itself became more diverse. By 1989, the total number of staff people representing diverse racial, ethnic, and national groups was 34 out of 85, or 40 percent. The board's cultural diversification task force decided the best way to implement its goals was through the establishment of a cultural diversification coordination group (co-group). AI volunteer co-groups had traditionally been ways to supplement staff research. We also decided to create a paid internship, the Ralph Bunche Fellows program, to provide a pipeline for young people interested in careers in human rights. Finally, we did targeted outreach to minority political and civil rights groups and made sure our expanded work on human rights education presented the work of figures like Bunche, Rosa Parks, and Martin Luther King, Jr.

In addition to this changing global context, two other developments spurred change in AIUSA. AI had begun its work against the death penalty in 1977, although executions in the United

Photo 18 Charles speaking at the Georgia death penalty march (1988)

States had been relatively rare since the Supreme Court's 1972 Furman decision. Popular support for the death penalty began to grow in the 1970s and 1980s. As executions in the US increased, especially after 1984, AIUSA ramped up its anti-death penalty work. Unlike prisoner cases in the US, in which the section could not participate, we were permitted to work against death penalty legislation and individual executions.

Our national death penalty campaigns had two consequences. Since half the inmates on death row were Black, in the eyes of the African American community, AIUSA now appeared to be concerned about human rights in this country. I, along with civil rights leaders Joseph Lowery and Coretta Scott King and Representatives John Conyers and John Lewis, spoke at the first anti-death penalty rally in Georgia on the steps of the state capitol in Atlanta, Georgia.

Photo 19 Charles at a death penalty press conference with John Lewis, Coretta Scott King, John Conyers, Joseph Lowry, and McKinley Young (1988)

AIUSA hired a Latino death penalty coordinator, Magdeleno Rose-Avila, and a Black regional director, Keith Jennings, based in Atlanta. This new visibility made it easier to recruit Black members.

A second consequence of our death penalty work was finding out what it was like to campaign for human rights in a hostile environment. When we went to churches and civic groups to ask them to write letters protesting the jailing of Soviet dissidents or sign petitions to stop torture in Turkey, we were greeted with open arms. Asking them to work to abolish the death penalty was another matter altogether. The common response was, "Why is AI working to put murderers back on the street?". We now knew what it was like for some of our members in countries hostile to human rights to campaign on issues such as gay rights and female genital mutilation. AIUSA's death penalty work also led some conservative members like William Buckley to leave the organization.

The second development that brought change to AIUSA was national rock concerts for human rights. Executive director Jack Healey, inspired by the success of the Secret Policeman's Ball in London in 1979 and the 1985 Live Aid concerts in London and Philadelphia, proposed a six-city "Conspiracy of Hope" tour across the United States in the summer of 1986 that would call for the release of six prisoners of conscience. At each stop, audiences would be asked to sign letters and perhaps even join AI. The purpose was to raise human rights awareness, not money.

Against all odds (nothing on this scale had been done for human rights), Healey, with the help of rock promoter Bill Graham and the support of the AIUSA board, put together a tour featuring U2, Sting, Peter Gabriel, Traci Chapman, and others (Bono's uncle Sean McBride was considered one of the founders of AI, so he was aware of our work). The tour culminated in a day-long concert at Giant's Stadium in New Jersey that was broadcast live on the new MTV network. As chair of AIUSA's board, I appeared on the broadcast to say a few words about our work. The program hosts were actor Donald Sutherland and comedian Richard Belzer. Just before my interview, I was bounced from my time slot by actor Christopher Reeve (aka Superman). I was asked to be ready to go on again and was again promptly bounced by New Jersey's governor. When I finally appeared, I'm pretty sure I was the only person in the stadium to be wearing a tie. The most disappointing part of the whole adventure, however, was missing my chance to meet Muhammad Ali. While I was doing my interview, he was introducing the next performer on stage and was gone before I got backstage. A photo of me and my guitar made the tour's program, but, fortunately for all concerned, I was not asked to play.

The tour raised over $2.6 million for the section and added 100,000 new members. The new members brought new energy and different ideas about diversity to our older base. In fact, the tour was so successful Healey proposed a worldwide human rights tour to the IEC in December 1986. There was a great deal of skepticism about whether such an ambitious project could work. A host of questions needed to be addressed, such as who would finance the tour, would IS resources be drained away from research to work on the tour, what countries would be visited, what would be the role of the section in each country, and finally, who would speak for the organization—the performers? All these issues required months of meetings, and I was involved in many of them.

Perhaps the most difficult issue to resolve was corporate sponsorship of the tour. We needed a corporation willing to underwrite about $2 million in upfront costs. It would be unthinkable to touch AI's program funding for such a risky undertaking. When Jack and I presented the idea of corporate sponsorship at an IEC meeting, the response was instantaneous and negative. The German and Dutch representatives were especially hostile. We told them that the "bake sale" model of raising funds that many sections used was simply inadequate for such a project. When we suggested that the Reebok corporation might be interested and would put a copy of the Universal Declaration of Human

Rights (UDHR) in each box of shoes it sold, the answer was a firm no. Imagine my surprise a few months later at another IEC meeting when the representative of one of those sections handed me an AI beer! He said they got a good deal from the brewer. How quickly the AI culture had changed. In the end, Healey formed a private concert corporation to shield AI from any liability.

The Human Rights Now! (HRN!) tour, marking the 40th anniversary of the UDHR and featuring Bruce Springsteen, Peter Gabriel, Sting, Youssou N'Dour, Traci Chapman, and others, kicked off in London on September 2, 1988, and concluded in Buenos Aires on October 15, 1988. In between, the tour visited France, Hungary, Italy, Spain, Costa Rica, Canada, the United States, Japan, India, Greece, Zimbabwe, Cote d'Ivoire, and Brazil. Multiple shows were held in the US, France, Canada, and Argentina to fund the cost of taking the tour to Asia, Africa, and South America while keeping ticket prices reasonable. It was suggested that I might want to hop on the plane with the rock stars for the whole tour; I declined, saying I had a day job and my dean might not appreciate me leaving for a month on a rock tour. I did participate in a pre-concert interview with television actress Holly Robinson in Philadelphia and took my family backstage for the concert in Oakland. A highlight for me was hearing 70,000 Argentinians singing "Biko" with Peter Gabriel at the last concert in Buenos Aires.

AIUSA's press officer and I also had the pleasure of staying overnight at Gabriel's home in Bath, England, during the planning stage of the tour. The HRN! Tour accomplished its mission of raising human rights awareness in the countries visited, adding new members to their groups and sections. Concertgoers produced

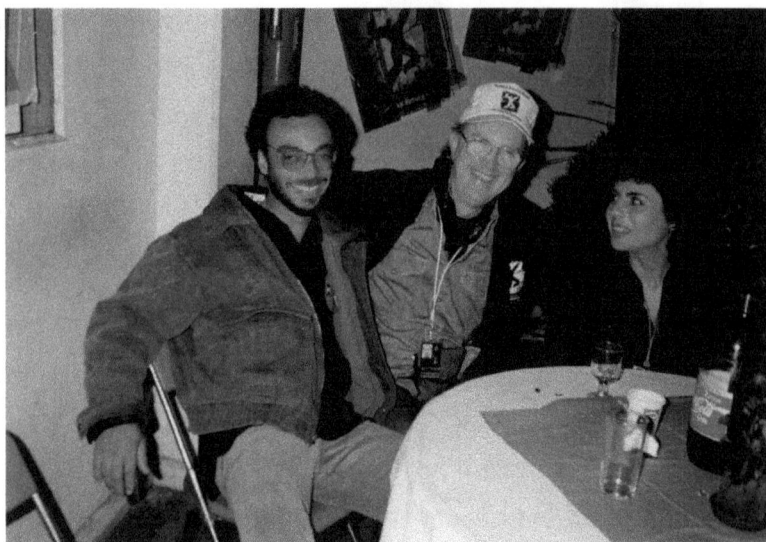

Photo 20 Charles backstage with Jack Healey and a friend in Buenos Aires (1988)

Photo 21 Charles at home with Peter Gabriel (1988)

tens of thousands of messages on behalf of Amnesty's prisoners of conscience and campaigns. Once again, young members brought new energy to the human rights movement.

If the HRN! Tour represented a high point of my international human rights experience, being elected to the IEC the following year turned out to be a low point. Despite the brief time I spent in places like Sierra Leone, most of my time was spent in long, contentious meetings at the IS in London. When Peter Behr of the Netherlands and I were elected to the IEC in Dublin, we joined a polarized group. With the one staff representative being neutral, the six other members were equally divided between those who wanted to renew the contract of Secretary General Ian Martin and those who wanted a new leader. The major complaint of the latter was that Martin had engaged in several actions without informing or gaining the consent of the IEC. Peter and I suggested giving Martin a one-year extension to work on specific areas of improvement like communications. As I recall, the extension happened but satisfied no one. Martin gained a new contract but left shortly afterward. By then I had been replaced on the IEC at the 1991 International Council Meeting (ICM) in Yokohama.

My two years on the IEC felt wasted. The workload was intense, the travel exhausting, and progress seemed minimal. Although the IEC was reasonably diverse, the two top leaders—the IEC chair Peter Duffy and Secretary General (SG) Martin—had been students at Cambridge at the same time and were often in conflict. The IS workplace culture seemed toxic, and the US section was regarded with suspicion. Perhaps the highlight of my visits to

Photo 22 Charles with the IEC (1990)

London was meeting AI's founders: Peter Benenson had started AI in 1961; Martin Ennals was the organization's first Secretary General; and Sean MacBride was the first IEC chair.

The modern human rights movement and I are about the same age and grew together. When the Universal Declaration of Human Rights (UDHR) was unanimously adopted by the UN General Assembly in 1948, with the Soviet Union, South Africa, and Saudi Arabia abstaining, there were roughly 50 recognized nations in the world. Some 800 million people still lived under colonialism, and all people were recovering from World War II. The formation of the UN, the drafting of the UDHR, and the various covenants and treaties that flowed from it gave hope to many that humanity could settle its differences through diplomacy and law rather than armed conflict.

In many ways the advent of the Cold War deadlocked meaningful action coming from the UN; however, the UDHR and human rights generally inspired anti-colonial movements abroad and the civil rights movement here in the United States. Peter Benenson was reportedly motivated by the example of American civil rights activists when he formed Amnesty International in 1961, just as I was inspired by them in 1960.

It was the proliferation of NGOs like AI in the 1960s and 1970s that gave real meaning to the abstract concept of human rights. With success came criticism. Some on the left argued human rights had replaced ideologies like socialism and communism that attacked structural inequality. Some on the right criticized human rights for intruding on national sovereignty. Yet both left and right have used human rights when it served their purpose.

Perhaps the most damaging charge has been that human rights are a Western concept that represents a type of neocolonialism. In my experience, that criticism almost always comes from those engaged in denying the rights of someone else. Moreover, to argue rights are a Western concept ignores the teachings of African and Eastern religions and philosophies from ancient times to the present. It also ignores the fact that governments from all regions and cultures have voluntarily signed human rights treaties.

It has been both a great challenge and a great privilege to build a mass, citizen-based human rights organization. I have met and worked with incredible people demanding their basic rights in hostile environments. It always amazed me that AI attracted such talented and dedicated staff for minimal wages and long hours.

Bill Schultz, AIUSA's former executive director, told me he had to institute a lights-out policy at 5 p.m. at their New York headquarters to keep staff from working late into the night. They were the opposite of power-hungry imperialists. For staff and volunteers, the reward was in the struggle. My Amnesty connections have led to my current position as Chair of the Board of the Center for Victims of Torture. In 2024, I visited the Kakuma refugee camp in Kenya and met with one of the 235,000 residents.

Photo 23 Charles with a Sudanese refugee (2024)

11
Global forums I

It was jarring to read in December 1993 that Secretary of State Warren Christopher had greeted PLO Head Yasser Arafat in the latter's headquarters in Rabat, Morocco. Six months earlier, in Vienna, Austria, United States delegates to the World Conference on Human Rights (WCHR) were not permitted to sit at the delegation's table in the General Assembly Hall when Arafat spoke. This was in keeping with the US practice of being officially absent whenever Arafat addressed the United Nations. Certainly, Arafat at the White House in September and Christopher in Rabat in December remind us how quickly events can shift on the world stage.

Global forums are stages or platforms on which governments and non-governmental organizations (NGOs), who are often the products of movements, meet on relatively equal terms. They are, in part, performative spaces but also hold the potential for actual change. While governments send delegations who debate each word of a treaty, covenant, or declaration before and during the meeting, the real energy comes from the NGOs who are often responsible for forcing the conference to be called. I attended meetings of the UN Human Rights Council in Geneva in the 1980s as an observer representing Amnesty International and as a delegate in the 1990s representing the United States government.

I found the proceedings formulaic. Most of the action occurred over which countries would sit on the Council, with each region of the world entitled to a certain number of seats. Once on the Council, it was predictable how they would vote on most human rights issues that would come to the floor. Every Council meeting would witness emotional but ritualistic debates over three perennial conflicts: Kashmir, Cuba, and Israel. Once the speeches were over, little seemed to change. I have also spoken at a UN Special Session Against Apartheid. Representing Amnesty International, my speech was sandwiched between those of New York Mayor David Dinkins and South African anti-apartheid leader Reverend Allan Boesak. Once again, the speeches and the outcome of the special session seemed predetermined. Global forums, however, presented more opportunities for progress; at least it appeared that way to me when I went as a delegate to the UN World Conference on Human Rights in Vienna in June 1993 and as an observer to the UN World Conference Against Racism (WCAR) in Durban, South Africa, in September 2001.

I flew to Vienna from JFK Airport on the same plane that carried former President Jimmy Carter. Carter greeted everyone on the plane and told me specifically that he was excited about being invited to address a plenary session of the NGOs on the last day of the pre-conference, where they hope to influence the conference agenda. It was a shock, then, to walk into the Assembly Hall a day later and find a major debate in progress on whether to let Carter speak. Perhaps because several other issues, including the representativeness of the NGO steering committee, were involved, no satisfactory solution was agreed on. Carter was belatedly brought onto the stage to a chorus of boos and hisses mixed with applause. After repeated attempts to speak over the noise, Carter asked the audience if they wanted him to continue. When most shouted yes, he went on, but the jeering did not cease. It was reportedly led by Latin American and Cuban NGO representatives who objected to Carter administration policies in their region.

This incident served to highlight the controversial role of United States leadership at the conference. After a period of 12 years in which the US government limited its human rights activity to a very narrow set of concerns and countries, the US delegation to Vienna was a high-profile one that gave daily press briefings and was actively engaged with both the NGOs and government delegations. The leader of the US delegation, Undersecretary of State Tim Wirth, had said that the US was shifting from bilateral to multilateral institutions but was hampered by the fact that we had not paid our dues to these institutions. On the issues, the US was moving into leadership on "non-helmet" issues like the environment, population growth, and human rights. We all expected cultural issues to be the most contentious at the conference. Although the US had been a strong proponent of having NGOs at the conference, a significant number of delegations and NGOs, including some from the United States, considered this country the leading purveyor of violence and human rights abuse in the world.

Given its unquestioned military dominance, it is understandable that more than a few countries regard any kind of action by the United States with caution. My role as a liaison between the official delegation and the NGOs was made difficult by several factors. First, the United States had to develop a coherent and fair policy in dealing with its own Indigenous peoples. One of the low points of the conference for me was explaining to a representative of an Indigenous peoples NGO that the US could not support a resolution to change the language of the Vienna document from "Indigenous people" to "Indigenous peoples". United States officials believed that the latter language might encourage American tribes to demand sovereignty. Second, the US needed to bring its own policies into compliance with accepted international standards. United States policy on Haitian refugees and Cuban detainees was repeatedly attacked at the conference. The open flouting of international law on these issues and others undercut any moral authority the United States might bring to the table. Third, the US government had to act on Secretary of State Christopher's promise to push for ratification of international human rights instruments. Specifically, Christopher promised to send to the Senate for action the Racial Convention, the Convention on Discrimination Against Women, and the International Covenant on Economic, Cultural and Social Rights, respectively. Fourth, the United States should listen to and work with African, Asian, and Latin American governments as co-equals. The attitude that the US and the West had a monopoly on human rights needed to cease. Only then could the United States exercise a global leadership role.

If the West ever needed any evidence that human rights were not solely a Western phenomenon, the appearance of the Dalai Lama at the conference was visible proof that it was not. While the Asian governments' regional preparatory meeting in Bangkok had put the issue of the universalism of human rights on the agenda, the real battle occurred not over language in the draft document but rather around the figure of the Dalai Lama. According to several reports, China had forced the UN to prohibit the Dalai Lama from speaking at the conference site to either the parallel conference of NGOs or the UN conference itself. Amnesty International (AI) rode to the rescue by inviting the Dalai Lama to make his address at its tent adjacent to the conference site.

Asian governments, led by China, were indeed the primary opponents of the major initiatives proposed in Vienna. However, it was not so much the banner of cultural relativism as political sovereignty that was raised to defend the status quo. As the incident with the Dalai Lama indicated, rights were not necessarily Western in that the religious leader constantly used them to promote his position. The Chinese could not argue that the Tibetans' cultural rights were being trampled by the West when in fact the Chinese were trampling them. They could and did use the time-honored argument that the UN had no political right to interfere in the domestic concerns of member nations. And, once again, it was an NGO (AI) and not the UN that proved itself resistant to governmental pressure on human rights activists by giving the Tibetan religious leader a forum.

A more visible threat to the universalism of human rights was not the traditional cultures of the Asian countries but rather their economic success. Specifically, the economic success of countries like South Korea, Singapore, and Taiwan (the Asian tigers) had provided the "third world" with an effective model of "authoritarian democracy" that gradually provided for increased political freedom. Despite the warning of AI's Secretary General

Pierre Sane that there was little difference between torture and starvation, the economic success of Southeast Asia was bidding to replace the discredited socialist model of Eastern Europe and the Soviet Union in many developing societies.

Not only was the socialist economic model discredited in the third world, but also the resolve of the West to deal with the human rights tragedy in its own backyard had helped undercut any sense of moral superiority. Only 200 miles north of Vienna lies the Bosnian border. Although the conference organizers had made every effort to keep country-specific items out of the debate, the location made such efforts futile. Bosnian Foreign Minister Haris Silajdzic asked, "Where is the political will?" and followed with a "demand of the participants, on behalf of humanity—because this is a crime against humanity—to take all measures to stop genocide in at least one town. Gorazde". He was given a standing ovation, a score of supportive speeches, and a resolution appealing to the UN Security Council to take the "necessary measures" to end the genocide in all of Bosnia. The United States was opposed to any country-specific resolutions being introduced because Bosnia would open the door for other country-specific resolutions, including Israel. This, in fact, happened as other country-specific resolutions poured forth; however, only Bosnia succeeded in getting a vote.

I split my conference time between official meetings and NGO meetings. I was the chair of the US delegation several times and was selected to be on the drafting committee for the final statement from the US. I was among old friends with many of the NGOs. I even ran across Vladimir Kartasken, who had been part of the USSR delegation to the Berkeley human rights dialogue in 1989. Vienna left me with two lasting impressions. The first is that human rights cut across all religious, cultural, social, and economic barriers when they serve the purpose of oppressed groups. In two of the most controversial events of the conference, the Dalai Lama and Bosnian Muslims appealed to the world on the basis of fundamental human rights. Even Peru's "Shining Path" had a table at the NGO forum.

The debate within the UN over human rights that has been dominated for so long by the confrontation between the Soviet Union and the United States is no more. During the conference, the US worked closely with delegates from the former Soviet republics, especially Russia and Ukraine, on several key issues. This debate has been replaced by a division between the global North and South best captured by the words of Nobel Laureate and former Nigerian political prisoner Wole Soyinka in his conference address. Soyinka said,

> on one side of the impassible gulf in the conference sat Power and its representatives, its champions; on the other side Freedom and its combatants. On the side of Freedom there were found some representatives of State. Those were the exceptions who had evolved gradually or been transformed suddenly. Those reformers guarded against the excesses of State. They were conscious of the pitfalls of Power. A contemporary example of that was the African National Congress through the voice of its leader Nelson Mandela.

Soyinka asked, how many of those who had been involved in a bitter war of liberation had the courage to admit that they had made mistakes? Such candor was a manifesto for a humane society and a rebuke to that other half, the praetorians of Power.

If the conference only partially achieved its goals, he continued, it was sufficient that the meeting had taken place and those on the other side of the impassable gulf had come to confront those in power. The conference, by giving voice to the victims of power, reminded all the participants that the victims of the powerful had not vanished. On the contrary, they were increasingly restless, as one bastion after another had fallen.

The United States moved toward closing the gap between the global North and South by recognizing the "right to development" and giving economic, cultural, and social rights equal priority with political and civil rights. Although much remained to be done to refine the US position on "development and democracy", this new stance won the country much goodwill among delegates from developing nations.

Another lasting impression of Vienna was the skill and success of the women's groups in making women's rights a priority issue. The Global Campaign for Women's Rights had been preparing for the conference for three years, and in the process, some 950 different women's organizations around the world backed the campaign. Evidence of their strength was the fact that much of the progressive language on women's rights in the conference working document was unbracketed (not open for debate). Pressure was kept on throughout the conference, culminating in a Global Tribunal on Violations of Women's Human Rights.

The United States delegation had as members two distinguished leaders in the struggle for women's rights, Geraldine Ferraro and

Arvonne Fraser. In her remarks to the main committee of the conference, Ferraro said, "Every day, women's rights as human beings are violated. When women are beaten, raped, and killed, as if it does not matter, they are denied their full humanity." She asked how can women be fully human when they receive less food, less medical care, less education, and more work than little boys. How can they be fully human when they cannot travel, vote, or control their own bodies? The United States supported the appointment of a special rapporteur on violence against women and the integration of women's concerns into every level of UN operations. Surely, the women's concerns provided strong evidence of the effectiveness of organized grassroots pressure and the cross-cutting nature of their human rights demands.

While a high commissioner for human rights and added resources for UN human rights work would undoubtedly increase the effectiveness of the UN's human rights efforts, they will not bridge the gulf between power and the champions for freedom. Only a massive growth of grassroots human rights organizations and inspired leadership will make the words of the Vienna document real.

Even more than Vienna, the WCAR in Durban was regarded by NGOs as a political opportunity to mobilize allies and shape public opinion. That opportunity is precisely why the United States opposed not only the WCAR in Durban but also two previous world conferences against racism. Despite its self-proclaimed role as a leader in racial justice, it was the rise of newly independent nations in Africa and Asia that demanded the UN act against racism. These "non-aligned", "third world", or "Global South" countries forced the UN between 1973 and 2003 to designate three decades of action to combat racism and racial discrimination. Midway through the first decade, in 1978, the first WCAR was convened in Geneva, Switzerland. The US opposed this conference because it specifically addressed the issue of apartheid in southern Africa. A decade later, the second WCAR was held in Geneva in 1983 to assess the progress made over the last ten years. This conference broadened its focus from apartheid to address discrimination against women, refugees, immigrants, and migrant workers. Once again, the US refused to participate.

When the UN decided in 1997 to call a third WCAR, there was a real question of whether the US would attend. There was no question, however, that US NGOs would attend both the conference and the preparatory committees (prepcoms), where much of the real work is done in setting the agenda and preparing a draft document (declaration). Five regional prepcoms were held across the globe. The regional meeting for the Americas was held in Santiago, Chile, in December 2000. I attended a meeting of the US NGO Coordinating Committee held in Oakland in the fall of 2000. It was at the prepcom meetings, especially the Americas regional meeting and the Africa regional meeting, that reparations rose as a central issue pitting Western governments against their own NGOs and the developing countries. The Canadian government objected to applying the modern legal concept of "crime against humanity" to acts that took place centuries ago. The US went further, suggesting that slavery might not be considered a crime. They preferred to focus on the current forms and manifestations of racism.

At the same time the NGO Coordinating Committee was created in the summer of 2000, the US government formed an interagency task force to plan American participation in the WCAR. The task force had its own series of meetings across the country, and it appeared as though the US would participate in a WCAR for the first time. While Secretary of State Colin Powell initially expressed enthusiasm for the conference, the prominence of reparations as an issue and the fear that Israel would be accused of apartheid led the US to withdraw its participation.

Despite the formal withdrawal of the US government, the call for reparations served to mobilize a constituency for collective action toward a political goal. A broad range of organizational types came together around the issue, including social movement organizations (SROs) like N'COBRA and the Leadership Conference on Civil Rights; supportive organizations such as colleges (e.g., Fisk) and church groups (e.g., United Church of Christ, Mennonite Church, Quakers); and even members of Congress (e.g., CBC). I attended the conference as a representative of the Meiklejohn Civil Liberties Institute based in Berkeley.

The unity behind a general call for reparations tended to mask the complexity of finding agreement from such a wide range of participants. At the regional meetings and prepcoms, an African/African Descendants Caucus was formed representing all the organizations supporting reparations. In daily meetings in Durban, different perspectives emerged and were debated. Most US participants saw the slavery issue as both a public apology and a precursor to reparations, while Latin American representatives tended to see reparations as also providing public recognition of special racial-group interests that would reinforce domestic politics. Most African representatives focused on reparations as potential redress for colonial exploitation. They were strongly opposed to an attack on modern-day slavery, upsetting delegates from Sudan and Mauritania. Afro-European representatives complained that the whole issue of reparations was too closely linked to African American interests. The fear of African American dominance was exacerbated by a speech Jesse Jackson delivered at a Durban town hall meeting. He said South African Blacks should use the US civil rights movement as an action model. Some of us thought that we were there to learn from African representatives, not lecture them on our past. After many discussions, the group issued its positions as "Ten Priority Action Points of Consensus", broadly reflective of all interest groups:

- The slave trade, slavery, and colonialism are crimes against humanity;
- Reparations for African and African Descendants;
- Recognition of the economic basis of racism;
- Adoption of corrective national (domestic) public policies with emphasis on environmental racism, health care, and education;
- Adoption of culture-specific development policies;
- The adoption of mechanisms to combat the interconnection of race and poverty and the role that globalization has in this interconnection;
- Adoption of mechanisms to combat racism in the criminal punishment (penal) system;

- Reform of the legal system, including national constitutional reforms and development of international and regional mechanisms for dismantling racism;
- Adoption of policies specific to African and African descendant women that recognize and address the intersection of race and gender; and
- Support for the adoption of policies that recognize and address the intersection of race and sexual orientation.

The final Durban Declaration and Programme of Action adopted by the WCAR draws heavily from the recommendations of the African/African Descendants Caucus of the NGO forum. In fact, it created a Permanent Forum on People of African Descent.

The rise of reparations at the Durban WCAR demonstrates the political opportunity created by global forums. In the four years of planning prior to Durban, there was no indication by governments that this topic would be a central issue. Certainly, the United States government used every opportunity available to derail reparations joined by a few African governments like Senegal and withdrew from the process when it could not control the outcome. NGOs, on the other hand, used the opportunity to network. Over the four years of meetings, a kind of Pan-African solidarity emerged based on reparations. While the attacks of September 11, two days after the close of the WCAR, served to shift the spotlight away from Durban and sidetrack the issue in the United States, the global reparations movement continued to grow. In the following years, American presidential candidates would be forced to address the issue; states and cities would develop their own plans; and countries such as France, the Netherlands, and Belgium began to repatriate African art and discuss compensation.

I saw some of the residual effects of Durban when I delivered a talk at a Caribbean Community (CARICOM) Pan-African conference in Barbados in 2003. Reparations were at the top of the agenda for the 15 member nations of the Caribbean region. Somewhat surprising given its strong British traditions, Barbados emerged as a center of regional Pan-African solidarity. In 2013, CARICOM launched a Reparations Commission that inspired the formation of the African American Reparations Commission, the European Reparation Commission, and similar groups in Canada and Great Britain, as well as national commissions in CARICOM nations. More recently, in July 2023, Barbados hosted a reparations conference with representatives from the African Union (AU) and CARICOM. Demands include an apology, debt cancellation, monetary compensation, and a host of educational and cultural programs. The following November, the African Union and the government of Ghana hosted the Accra Reparations conference. Of course, African and Caribbean nations are demanding reparations from the former colonial powers while African Americans are making demands on their own government. Still, the reparations movement represents the largest expression of Pan-African solidarity since the movement to end apartheid in southern Africa.

12
Global forums II

In July 1987, Ninel Streltsova of the Novosti Press Agency phoned Bert Gross from Moscow to invite him to take part in the first international panel on human rights to be held in the Soviet Union (USSR). After explaining the structure of the panel, she assured him that under Gorbachev's *glasnost* and *perestroika*, Gross would find the USSR very different from what he had observed when visiting there in 1972 on behalf of the United Nations.

Since I had been working closely with Bert on his attempts to revive full employment legislation in the United States Congress, I was quickly drafted by him to work on a new US–USSR human rights dialogue. Bert had been tutoring me on his efforts to implement full employment legislation in the US since the New Deal. I, in turn, had been briefing Bert on my work to implement various human rights treaties and conventions with Amnesty International. The result had been a broader approach to full employment that manifested itself in concrete form as the "Economic Bill of Rights Act" introduced in Congress by Representatives Charles Hayes and Augustus Hawkins.

As the only US participant in this two-day panel in Moscow, Bert was asked what would make *glasnost* and *perestroika* more credible in the West. Bert's reply stressed the importance of Soviet withdrawal from Afghanistan, allowing free emigration, and releasing "prisoners of conscience". Of course, the Soviets were interested in Bert because of his work on economic rights, but none of the Soviet panelists disagreed with his views on political and civil rights. Perhaps there *was* an opportunity to begin a new East–West human rights dialogue.

The kind of global or transnational dialogue we envisioned was different from international forums like Davos that involve economic actors and corporations. It could also be distinguished from scientific or technical meetings of professionals around such issues as climate change and space exploration. The proposed dialogue would even be different than the UN's human rights and racial discrimination forums because the official participants would not be government delegations. What was being proposed has been labeled a transnational advocacy network distinguishable largely by the centrality of principled ideas or values in motivating their formation. Such networks are communicative structures, but they are also political spaces in which differently situated actors hope to shape or influence those with political power.

Bert's visit to Moscow quickly led to a proposed joint USA–USSR book on the future of human rights in the two countries, co-edited by Bert and Avgust Mishin, professor of law at Moscow State University and chair of the panel.

Returning from the Moscow discussions, Bert sent out a Gross–Mishin book outline to an expanding list of American scholars and a few public figures, asking for substantive comments. Some 90 responses were received, with most in favor of seizing this window of opportunity. As it became clear that face-to-face meetings would be necessary to advance the project, a small planning meeting was held at Berkeley in March 1988, supported by my department, Afro-American Studies, and the Peace and Conflict Studies program. An improved working paper emerged from this meeting along with the idea for a major Berkeley conference. After more networking by Bert at the Soviet-American Citizens Summit in Virginia and an intensive visit to the USSR by Peter Juviler of Columbia University in the spring of 1988, the stage was set for "Human Rights and the Future: An Open Forum", a USSR–USA Scholar's Dialogue on Human Rights held at Berkeley on August 10–11, 1989, under the auspices of the American Council of Learned Societies and the USSR Academy of Sciences.

The conference proceedings revolved around two central questions—what are the opportunities for and obstacles to significant progress in the two countries? Historically, the United States had given priority to negative rights—that is, prohibitions limiting governments' control over the individual. The Soviet Union, on the other hand, emphasized the role the state could play in granting economic, social, and cultural rights, for example, positive rights. In addition to the human rights scholars on the program, other US participants included the Assistant Secretary of State for Human Rights and Humanitarian Affairs Richard Schifter, ACLU President Norman Dorson, Representative Augustus Hawkins, and C. W. Poircer of the American Bar Association. The Soviet scholars included Elena Lukasheva, Viktor Chkhikvadze, Aleksandr Kabalken, Vladimir Kartashkin, and Irina Ledyakh—all from the human rights division of the Institute for State and Law. Other Soviet participants were Nobel Prize-winning physicist

Andrei Sakharov and his wife, Dr Elena Bonner. Facing an admiring audience of over 1,000, Sakharov said, "We need to radicalize perestroika. To do that, there needs to be assistance from the West—pressure brought to bear so that people see that cooperation with the Soviet Union is feasible and with the Chinese workable. Otherwise, a turn backwards will be a disaster for all." In a remark aimed at Berkeley leftists, Bonner added that "you must understand that socialism, except for the utopia in books, produced nothing as far as the people are concerned."

I moderated a televised roundtable on the first evening of the conference and, with Professor Essie Seck of USC, was responsible for meeting with the discussion leaders of each panel and troubleshooting any problems along with conference administrator Dr Rita Maran. Fortunately, the conference went smoothly, with the appearance of Sakharov and Bonner drawing a lot of press coverage. The initial book proposal soon expanded into a major work including both prominent scholars and public figures, from former President Jimmy Carter and state department officials to the president of the AFL-CIO. Everyone agreed, however, that the work should be geared to a general audience rather than scholars. The publication of the book to be entitled *Human Rights and the Future* was to occur in 1991 before the Moscow International Conference on Human Rights and Humanitarian Cooperation. Further meetings were planned on the themes of 1. political and nationality rights (1990 in Moscow), 2. economic, social, and cultural rights (1991 in the US), and 3. human rights and international relations (USSR in 1992).

The next year, the follow-up conference on political and nationality rights was held at the Institute of State and Law in Moscow from June 17 to 24, 1990. Bert and I were in a US delegation that included James Nickel, Rhoda Howard, Hurst Hannum, Ron Takaki, James Anaya, Peter Juviler, Frank Bonilla, and Bert Lockwood.

Prior to arriving in Moscow, I enjoyed a few days as a tourist in St. Petersburg. My brother, Oren, had planned to join me but could not get a visa. After arriving at my hotel from the airport, imagine my surprise in opening the door and hearing M. C. Hammer's "You Can't Touch This" coming from a hotel restaurant rather than Russian music. The weather was also a surprise. Even though it was June, my jacket provided little comfort in the cold air. After visiting the Hermitage and a few other sites, I took an over-night train to Moscow from the same station Lenin arrived at in January 1917 from Germany. The station had a full assortment

Photo 24 US delegation to USSR human rights dialogue in Moscow (1990)

of characters, including one who asked me if Lake Oswego was in California and another who offered me a swig of whatever he was drinking. I declined, and he poured himself a drink in an old ceramic cup and reacted so strongly that I knew I would have died if I had joined him. We pulled out at 11:33 pm with Nat King Cole on my headset and still enough light in the sky to read without a lamp.

I took a taxi to the accommodations arranged by our hosts, reportedly a former mental institution. Fortunately, that was not an omen, as the meetings at the Institute of State and Law with most of the scholars we met at Berkeley were productive. We made progress on the proposed joint book and looked forward to another meeting in Berkeley. Moreover, I had time to visit a few of Amnesty's human rights contacts in Moscow. One contact was a distinguished 90-year-old physicist and his daughter and her husband, who lived in the Petrograd district. He had been a pioneer in radio waves and had a larger apartment than most Russians—four rooms. His granddaughter served my colleague and me a great meal including wine and vodka, although they were concerned that I didn't eat much. I had just finished a large lunch at Pushkin's "Literary" café. The granddaughter would like to visit the US but found it too difficult to get tickets (800 rubles). She must go to apply every Wednesday. As a medical doctor, she makes 179 rubles a month ($17) less than the Soviet average of 250 rubles.

Her story was like that of the professionals I had lunch with. Both had limited opportunities because they were Jewish. Antisemitism was on the rise, and they wanted a better life for their nine-year-old daughter. Decisions had been made to go to

Israel, but the wife had to stay to care for her 85-year-old grand-mother. She said she would study Yiddish and wait.

Unfortunately, our plans for further meetings were disrupted the following year when Gorbachev was removed from power, and the book was never produced. Bert and Peter Juviler did co-edit a book on *Human Rights for the 21st Century* in 1993, which con-tained some of the thinking around the dialogue. I contributed a piece on human rights education.

Bert's stepdaughter, Gayatri Singh, a human rights lawyer in India, arranged for my participation in a "National Conference on Human Rights, Social Movements, Globalization and the Law" in Panchgani, India, in December 2000. It provided another oppor-tunity to see how human rights were being used by activists, lawyers, judges, and media in a different cultural context.

A different window of opportunity opened in 1993 when I was elected president of the National Council for Black Studies (NCBS). Amnesty International and human rights had taken a good deal of my time, and I looked forward to resuming my efforts to promote and expand Black Studies nationally. However, upon assuming the presidency, it quickly became clear that NCBS had an oppor-tunity to grow internationally. Specifically, two members of the executive committee, Selase Williams and Bill Little, along with executive director Jacqui Wade, had prepared to hold an NCBS administrative summer workshop in Accra, Ghana. Although the workshops were funded by the Ford Foundation, we decided it would be possible to do an international Black Studies con-ference at the University of Legon in Ghana in the summer of 1994. To my knowledge, it was the first-ever global conference of Black Studies scholars. American participants included John Hendrik Clarke, Maya Angelou, Maulana Karenga, Wade Nobles, Ray Winbush, Barbara Sizemore, and others. Along with our host, Ghanaian scholars, former Zambian President Kenneth Kaunda, and Kenyan novelist Ngugi wa Thiong'o participated. The conference opened at the new national theater (built by the Chinese) with a speech by the minister of education. I was surprised when he pulled me aside after the speech to ask for my help in introducing Afro-centric education in Ghana's schools! He said students' final examinations were sent to England for grading, and most of their literature consisted of English classics. I put him in touch with some of our participants who had designed Afro-centric curricula. I had had my own frustrating experience as a member of an advisory board to the Oakland school district when it was dealing with choosing a multicultural history textbook and the subject of "Black English". Getting him help for the new technical school in Kumasi proved less successful. It was offering no courses in computer science due to the lack of computers in Ghanaian secondary schools, and my efforts with Apple failed to produce any results. For many African American participants, including me, the most emotional highlight of the conference was a trip to Cape Coast Castle. Cape Coast was a fort/prison that held enslaved Africans until ships arrived to transport them to the Americas. Looking out over the ocean from the door of no return is something I will never forget. We were also surprised at the rather small museum with limited information at Cape Coast. The museum guide explained that the period of the slave trade was not one Ghanaians were proud of or wanted to remember.

Another highlight was a visit to the tomb of W. E. B. DuBois, where there is a small museum. DuBois is considered the intellectual father of Black Studies and spent the last few years of his long life as the honored guest of the Ghanaian government while working on an *Encyclopedia Africana*. It was bittersweet to see DuBois accorded the recognition in Ghana that had been denied him in the United States.

The Ghanaian government recognized the significance of the conference by granting the NCBS leadership a meeting with President Jerry Rawlings.

Rawlings was quite candid in his remarks to the group, telling us a story about the baptism of his children. Rawlings was Catholic and met with the bishop in Accra to arrange for a baptism

Photo 25 NCBS leadership meeting with President Rawlings (1994)

ceremony. The bishop informed him that his children could not be baptized because they had African names. When Rawlings protested that they were Christian, the bishop insisted they needed English names for the ceremony to take place!

At our final banquet, I was pleased to sit between poet Maya Angelou and President Kaunda to pick their brains. Angelou had been part of a small group of Black Americans that had relocated to Ghana after it gained independence in 1960. Although Angelou returned to the United States, the group of Black expatriates still existed. In fact, the head of the group, ironically a dentist named Robert Lee, approached me about NCBS assuming responsibility for a former slave fort now controlled by the expatriates. I had to tell him that unfortunately, like his group, we had no resources to maintain such a structure. The dinner ended with me being "enstooled" by the minister of culture. I gave the beautiful stool to NCBS, but I did buy a large painting for my wife for our 25th wedding anniversary by local artist and art professor Ablade Glover. It hangs in our living room, reminding me of the Ghana homecoming.

The Ghana conference was successful enough to lead me to believe we could pull off another international conference—this time in South America. Given that a majority of enslaved Africans landed in the Caribbean and South America rather than the United States, the location made sense. The problem was that NCBS had no good contacts with institutions south of the border. Fortunately, my Berkeley colleague Percy Hintzen, a native of Guyana, had taken a leave to work with the president of Guyana and the vice-chancellor of the University of Guyana. When I contacted Percy, he immediately agreed to lay the groundwork for holding our next NCBS annual meeting in Guyana. After several failed attempts to reach Percy at his cousin's home by telephone, I decided to make a planning trip to Georgetown, the capital. Every time I had called Percy, even late at night, his cousin had said he was at the library. When Percy picked me up at the airport after a long flight from San Francisco, he said, let's stop by the library before you go to your hotel. I replied that it was late, and I was too tired to go to the library. Percy laughed and said the library is a nightclub and we should have a drink to celebrate your arrival!

Percy told me that a group of protestors had threatened to demonstrate at the conference because we had received funds from the Ford Foundation. They had backed down when Percy threatened to expose them for receiving funds from the lumber industry. Despite this incident, Percy said plans for the conference were proceeding smoothly. I, however, was a bit concerned about security. When I arrived at the top hotel in Georgetown, I asked the desk clerk for directions for a walk along the waterfront. He suggested that I might want to rethink a walk because of the possibility of pirates in the bay!

Our NCBS conference kicked off a few months later with an opening plenary at the National Theater. I was on stage to welcome the conference participants to Guyana. Percy was on stage to introduce our speaker, Cheddi Jagan, the president of Guyana. Due to Percy's help, the government had given us a small grant, and Jagan hosted a reception for NCBS participants. The president began his remarks with a concise history of Pan-Africanism and made special mention of DuBois and Paul Robeson. His speech was well-received until he began to criticize the previous administration. Jagan had been elected president two years earlier on the People's Progressive Party ticket with the almost total support of the Indo-Guyanese population. The losing People's National Congress Reform Party of Forbes Burnham was almost totally composed of the Afro-Guyanese population. They had controlled the country since independence in 1966 and made up most of our audience that evening. Forbes Burnham, who was in the audience, walked out and took most of the audience with him. We quickly closed the session with the few remaining audience members. The next morning the national newspaper ran a front-page story on the conference with the headline "No Blacks on Stage at Black Studies Conference". When I protested to Percy, he said, look Jagan is Indo-Guyanese, I'm Dougla (mixed race), and in Guyanese eyes, you're White!

After this newsworthy opening, it was no surprise that our keynote speaker, Black psychologist and socialist Lenora Fulani, was controversial. She had run for president of the United States in 1988 and 1992 on the New Alliance Party ticket, and her leftist politics were closer to those of Jagan than Burnham.

At our banquet, NCBS sought to honor the Guyanese scholar, the late Walter Rodney, author of *How Europe Underdeveloped Africa*. Rodney's brother had come to receive the award, and when I presented it to him, he launched into a speech attacking both the current administration and the previous administration for not properly investigating his brother's death. Since I was sitting between Jagan's prime minister and Burnham, the situation became tense. Fortunately, he sat down before anything happened. After a stop at the library to say goodbye to Percy's students, I was happy to head home the next day.

In 1995, Berkeley hosted the NCBS annual meeting for the second time. The conference was historic in that we were able to hold joint sessions with the Asian American Studies Association and the Chicano Studies Association. It was one of the few times when I could say things in Berkeley were calmer than in our previous locations. At the end of my presidency, I could say that our network of Black scholars had grown both internationally and domestically, and I had grown from teaching Black Studies at Newark High School to taking it to Berkeley, Accra, and Georgetown.

13
Conclusion

"There is a prophet within us, forever whispering that behind the seen lies the immeasurable unseen."
Frederick Douglass

In the wake of President Andrew Johnson's generous policy of pardons to ex-Confederates and his returning of much confiscated and abandoned lands to their former Southern owners, Congress called a halt to presidential Reconstruction. Responding to reports of repeated violence against the formerly enslaved, Congress passed a new Freedman's Bureau bill and the Fourteenth Amendment to the Constitution.

During the hearing on this legislation, a group of Black men and one White man led by Frederick Douglass demanded a meeting with President Johnson. Addressing the president, Douglass said, "In the order of Divine Providence you are placed in a position where you have the power to save or destroy us, to bless or blast us". In an angry and rambling 45-minute response, Johnson replied he was ready to be "the Moses" of the freed people and declared that "the feelings of my own heart… have been for the colored man". As proof, he stated that he had owned slaves and bought slaves but never sold one. Johnson then complained that in his relationship with Blacks, "I have been their slave instead of their being mine. Some even followed me here, while others are occupying… my property with my consent." However, Johnson feared a race war if his Black guests pursued their goals of equal treatment and suffrage. He believed colonization remained the best option for freed people. The president urged Douglass to consider the plight of poor non-slaveholding Whites who had been kept poor during slavery by the colored man and master (Blight, 2018, pp. 473–475).

Douglass must have had a sense of deja vu. In an 1862 meeting between President Lincoln and Black leaders, Lincoln seemed to blame the war on the presence of Blacks. "But for your race among us there could not be war, although many men engaged on either side do not care for you one way or another. Slavery had had evil effects on the White race, the president said, and racial equality could never be possible in America. Lincoln told the Black delegation that it was "extremely selfish" of them to reject his pleas for voluntary repatriation to a foreign country." He concluded, "it is exceedingly important that we have men at the beginning capable of thinking as white men and not those who have been systematically oppressed." (Ibid., p. 371). Thus, we have what many historians consider the worst and the best American president agreeing that Whites are the true victims of slavery and that if Blacks really knew what was good for them, they would leave the country of their birth.

The current American president, Donald Trump, is fond of comparing himself favorably with Lincoln. Trump does share with Lincoln and Johnson a belief in White supremacy and the conviction that Whites are the true victims of the Black presence. However, within a year of his meeting with Douglass and other Black leaders, Lincoln would respond to the pressure of the abolitionist movement and the exigencies of war with the Emancipation Proclamation. By providing a moral imperative for the Civil War, Lincoln laid the foundation for a second republic best expressed in the Gettysburg Address. Despite Andrew Johnson's protests, this new founding included Blacks as citizens, as reflected in the Thirteenth, Fourteenth, and Fifteenth Amendments to the Constitution as well as the Civil Rights Act of 1866.

Of course, Johnson's vision of a country returned to its pre-Civil War status, minus the institution of slavery, did not die. The end of the so-called "radical Reconstruction" saw the re-emergence of the old South based on sharecropping with the old racial order enforced by White terrorist groups like the Ku Klux Klan. Segregation, separate and unequal, whether de facto as in the North or de jure as in the South, remained dominant until the civil rights movement of the post-World War Two era. Built on the legacies of Douglass, Sojourner Truth, Martin Luther King, Fannie Lou Hamer, and many others, the activists of my generation sought to fulfill the promise of a multiracial, pluralistic democracy. They challenged White identity politics with Black, Brown, and Feminist power. Civil rights broadened to include a more expansive human rights perspective. Symbolically, this new or third republic culminated with the election of Barack Obama.

Donald Trump's political rise coincided with the rejection of a multiracial, pluralistic democracy by large numbers of Americans. Trump built a political following by denying the citizenship and religion of Obama. The establishment of the Tea Party at the outset of the Obama administration signaled the formalization of this resistance just as the rise in hate crimes and the January 6 insurrection marked the informal resistance. Trump's election as president on a platform featuring anti-immigration policies and the defeat of Hillary Clinton ended the second radical Reconstruction.

With Trump's re-election in 2020, he has not only sought to consolidate political power on an unprecedented scale but also challenged the power of civil society (moral authority) and the institutions of knowledge (expert authority). Having given up the pursuit of a political career early in my life, I have pursued social justice through work in civil society institutions and academic institutions. Consequently, I have seen firsthand the damage Trump's actions are causing. Led by the world's richest human, Elon Musk, the gutting of USAID has hurt the lives of many of the world's poorest people. The non-governmental organization (NGO) I chaired until 2025, the Center for Victims of Torture (CVT), provided mental health services and security to those fleeing persecution and torture around the world. In February 2024, I traveled to Kenya and visited CVT clients in safe houses and refugee camps who told me our organization had saved their lives. A year later, our doors are closed and staff are laid off due to the suspension of federal grants. Even in the governmental sector, the office I directed in the State Department in the mid-1990s promoting democracy building has had its funding suspended. These programs fought corruption rather than embracing it.

This attack on humanitarian and human rights organizations has moved in parallel with an attack on the institutions of education from kindergarten through graduate school. Expertise or scientific authority represents another threat to political power.

It follows that the Trump administration has sought to weaken and hinder the institutions and organizations that exercise such authority. From controlling the K-12 curriculum as in his 1776 project on patriotic education to the defunding of the National Science Foundation and National Health Institute, Trump is undermining scientific authority. Of course, this effort is global in withdrawing from the International Climate Accords and the World Health Organization.

Attacks on Diversity, Equity, and Inclusion (DEI) and critical race theory have led the charge because they are softer targets than health research or astrophysics. DEI has been blamed for the Los Angeles fires and the Washington, DC, plane crash with no evidence. At the same time, grossly incompetent Whites have been placed in charge of national security and health. It is a raw assertion of political power over knowledge with potentially frightening consequences.

Black studies, Ethnic Studies, and Gender Studies have been under attack since their creation in the 1960s and 1970s. They have always been underfunded and marginalized on college campuses. In my experience as a faculty equity officer, it was only the promise of additional resources that would move traditional disciplines to consider minority and female colleagues. Now that the well-funded sciences are under attack, perhaps they will join their poverty-stricken cousins in humanities and social sciences in resisting this assault on academic freedom.

The movement for the abolition of slavery was the first global human rights movement. It involved women and men of various races, faiths, and flaws working through a variety of sacred and secular organizations. To recall that struggle is to draw hope and insight into ways we might protect and advance social justice. Justice, as Martin Luther King and Reinhold Niebuhr remind us, is the best we can hope for as a collective. That is, relationships between groups are basically political and not ethical. We can love individuals, but the best we can hope for between groups is fairness and justice. Moreover, the egoism of social groups is greater than that of individuals. It is this egoism that leads to the constant struggle between "we" and "them".

Our life as a nation has been a constant struggle to define "we" as a people. It has been a battle across many platforms between those promoting a broadly inclusive "we" and those seeking a narrow, exclusive "we". Obviously, Andrew Johnson and Trump represent the exclusive definition of our nation in their promotion of White male patriarchy and attacks on immigrants and the Fourteenth Amendment. Although Trump is willing to expand his notion of "we" to include Greenlanders and Canadians but not Mexicans. Frederick Douglass and Obama represent a more inclusive vision of America best expressed by poet Langston Hughes in the first three stanzas of his "Let America be America Again":

> Let America be America again.
> Let it be the dream it used to be.
> Let it be the pioneer on the plain
> Seeking a home where he himself is free.
> (America never was America to me.)
> Let America be the dream the dreamers
>   dreamed—
> Let it be that great strong land of love

Where never kings connive nor tyrants scheme
That any man be crushed by one above.
(It never was America to me.)
O, let my land be a land where Liberty
Is crowned with no false patriotic wreath,
But opportunity is real, and life is free,
Equality is in the air we breathe.
(There's never been equality for me,
Nor freedom in this "homeland of the free".)

(Hughes, 1990)

Related to this constant struggle for inclusion is the notion of change as the only constant. There can never be a return to a "golden age" or, as Douglass says, the unseen future. A major reason why the study of politics is more of an art form than a science is the unpredictability of human nature. In the world of politics, enemies might be friends one day and enemies the next. Economics has avoided the problem of human decision-makers by assigning decisions to an impersonal market. Pragmatism in politics and a market economy may seem the best way forward, but they lack moral imperative. That is, they avoid the question of value.

When I taught public policy, I always used a work by Richard Nelson entitled *The Moon and the Ghetto*. Nelson asks the question of why we can reach the moon but not solve the problems of the ghetto. A short answer is to follow the money. But a longer answer involves why we as a society decide that something is a problem and why we decide it must be solved. It raises the question of whether we value some lives more than others. King was fond of pointing out the difference between desegregation and integration. Desegregation was a negative action in that it prohibited acts of discrimination. Integration, on the other hand, required positive action. It required the positive acceptance of desegregation and the welcome participation of Blacks in the total range of human activities. In the words of the philosopher Richard Rorty, human rights require the gradual expansion of the notion of empathy. If we can see ourselves as the other, we can come to accept that they have all the rights that we have.

Discussion questions

- What is a movement? How do they become institutionalized?
- Can an individual have an identity apart from a group?
- Can groups of unequal power form effective coalitions?
- Are all rights of equal importance? If not, how do you prioritize them?
- Are human rights universal?
- What is objectivity? What is knowledge?

Bibliography

Blight, D. W. (2018). *Frederick Douglass*. New York: Simon & Schuster.

Chisholm, S. (1973). *The Good Fight*. New York: Harper & Row.

Halisi, C. and Mtume, J. (eds.) (1967). *The Quotable Karenga*. Los Angeles. US.

Hayward, C. (2013). *How Americans make race*. New York: Cambridge University Press

Henry, C. P. (ed.) (2011). *The Obama Phenomenon*. Urbana, IL: University of Illinois Press.

Henry. C. P. (1991). *Jesse Jackson*. Oakland, CA: The Black Scholar Press.

Hughes, L. (1990). *Selected Poems of Langston Hughes*. New York: Vintage.

Macaluso, L. (2018). *Guide to Thomas Jefferson's Virginia*. Charleston, SC: Arcadia Publishing.

Malcomson, S. (2000). *One Drop of Blood*. New York: Farrar, Straus and Giroux.

McMillan, F. P. (2002). *Locating the Neo-black Aesthetic*. Chapel Hill, NC: University of North Carolina Press.

Moses, W. J. (1998). *Afrotopia*. New York: Cambridge University Press.

Newton, H. (n.d.). *Essays From the Minister of Defense*. Oakland, CA: Black Panther Party.

Painter, N. I. (2006). *Creating Black America*. New York: Oxford University Press.

Washington, J. M. ed. (1986). *A Testament of Hope.* New York: Harper & Row.

Weiner, D. E. (2013). *Race and Rights.* DeKalb, IL: Northern Illinois University Press.

Additional reading

Drake, S. C. (1987). *Black folk here and there*. Los Angeles, CA: UCLA Center for Afro American Studies.

Henry, C. P. (2017). *Black Studies and the Democratization of American Higher Education*. New York: Palgrave Macmillan.

Keck, M. E., and Sikkink, K. (1998). *Activists Beyond Borders*. Ithaca, NY: Cornell University Press.

Levine, L. (1977). *Black Culture and Black Consciousness*. New York: Oxford University Press.

Nelson, R. R. (1977). *The Moon and the Ghetto*. New York: Norton.

Singh, N. P. (2004). *Black is a country*. Cambridge, MA: Harvard University Press.

Index